Mori Arinori's
Life and Resources in America

STUDIES OF MODERN JAPAN

Series Editor: Edward R. Beauchamp, University of Hawaii

Studies of Modern Japan is a multidisciplinary series that consists primarily of original studies on a broad spectrum of topics dealing with Japan since the Meiji restoration of 1868. Additionally, the series aims to bring back into print classic works that shed new light on contemporary Japan. In all cases, the goal is to publish the best scholarship available, by both established and rising scholars in the field, in order to better understand Japan and the Japanese during the modern period and into the future.

Editorial Advisory Board

Titles in the Series

Mori Arinori's
Life and Resources in America

Edited, annotated, and introduced by
John E. Van Sant

Foreword by Akira Iriye

LEXINGTON BOOKS
Lanham • Boulder • New York • Toronto • Oxford

LEXINGTON BOOKS

Published in the United States of America
by Lexington Books
An imprint of The Rowman & Littlefield Publishing Group, Inc.
4501 Forbes Boulevard, Suite 200, Lanham, Maryland 20706

PO Box 317
Oxford
OX2 9RU, UK

British Library Cataloguing in Publication Information Available

Library of Congress Cataloging-in-Publication Data

Mori, Arinori, 1847–1889.
   [Life and resources in America]
   Mori Arinori's life and resources in America / edited, annotated, and
introduced by John E. Van Sant.
           p. cm.
Includes bibiographical references and index.
   ISBN 0-7391-0605-8 (cloth : alk. paper) — ISBN 0-7391-0793-3 (pbk. :
alk. paper)
   1. United States—Description and travel. 2. United
States—Civilization—1865–1918. 3. United States—Foreign public
opinion, Japanese. I. Title: Life and resources in America. II. Van
Sant, John E., 1958– III. Title.
   E168.M85 2004
   973.5—dc29

                                                      2003019644
Printed in the United States of America

⊗™ The paper used in this publication meets the minimum requirements of American
National Standard for Information Sciences—Permanence of Paper for Printed Library
Materials, ANSI/NISO Z39.48-1992.

Contents

Note on Japanese Names

Japanese names in the foreword and the introduction are in traditional Japanese order: family name first and given name second. For example, "Mori" is a family name and "Arinori" is a given name. This is not always the case, however. Mori himself often used the Western order of given name first and family name second when writing in English. Footnotes, endnotes, and the bibliography are in Western bibliographic style.

Foreword

When we think of foreign observations about the United States in the nineteenth century, such names as Alexis de Tocqueville, Harriet Martineau, Karl Marx, and James Bryce come to mind. Their writings on aspects of American society, politics, and culture have made lasting impressions on readers both in the United States and abroad. It is no exaggeration to say that we gain a deeper understanding of American history and the American people by seeing how perceptive visitors from abroad have sought to make sense of them — and to relate the American experience to global developments.

Virtually all foreign observers of the United States that we are familiar with, however, come from Europe. This is true not just of nineteenth-century but also of twentieth-century accounts. A few visitors from such "extra-European" countries as Canada and Australia have published their travel accounts of the nation, but we know little about the writings by visitors who have come to the United States from Asia, the Middle East, Africa, or Latin America. Only a tiny handful of them has been written and published in English. A very useful anthology, *From the Outer World*, edited by Oscar and Lilian Handlin, contains fascinating excerpts from some of these writings.[1] The bulk of non-European observations about the United States remains untranslated. For those interested in Japanese perspectives on the United States, Peter Duus has published a very useful volume, *The Japanese Discovery of America*, containing a collection of essays on the United States by Japanese writers in the nineteenth century.[2] A recent translation of Nagai Kafū's *Amerika monogatari* (American stories) has made available in English a significant opus by one of Japan's foremost literary figures at the turn of the twentieth century.[3] Other than these examples, there is a real paucity of translated material, despite the fact that literally hundreds of books about the

ix

United States have been written by Japanese since the "opening" of the country a century and a half ago. Under the circumstances, the publication of a new edition of Mori Arinori's *Life and Resources in America* is welcome news.

This book, it is true, is not a translation of a Japanese publication. It was written and published in English, and as the editor, John Van Sant, notes, it has never been available in Japanese. Even so, it would be safe to assume that Mori must have first penned his thoughts in Japanese and then, with the assistance of Charles Lanman (a well-known American writer on Japan in the middle of the nineteenth century) and others, produced the English-language version. Although he was in the United States at that time and is known to have developed remarkable skills in writing English prose, it is difficult to see how he could have composed the text with its often colloquial style. Moreover, the vast array of statistical data and detailed information concerning local history and geography in which the volume abounds could have been gathered only with the help of research assistants. Even so, there is no denying the fact that Mori published what may be considered the first comprehensive account of American politics, society, and culture written by a Japanese.

By the time the book was first published in late 1871, Tocqueville's *Democracy in America* had been around for more than thirty years, as had Harriet Martineau's *Society in America*. Mori may or may not have read these and other books. Unlike them, he does not indulge in the use of the first person singular, so that it is not always clear if what he is reporting is based on his personal observations or on information obtained from books and other sources. Mori's work is more encyclopedic than the European authors'; he touches on, and gives brief descriptions of, the politics, economy, education, religion, art, geography, and society of the United States so that the overall impression one gets is that it is more an objective survey than a personal and interpretive essay. This does not make the book less interesting, however, since its very organization and contents reflect Mori's view of what would be of value to Japanese readers, assuming that the volume would be read by his countrymen, in translation if not in the original. Moreover, the volume shares a number of themes with the writings by Tocqueville, Martineau, and other European visitors to the United States. For instance, they all believe that what is taking place in the United States is a harbinger of things to come in other countries. For this very reason, they are struck by the contrast between American self-perception (i.e., the ideals for which the people stood) and the reality, especially with regard to race prejudice and political corruption. Mori seems to be particularly intrigued by the gap between Christian doctrine that the majority of the American people profess and their actual conduct. Tocqueville's stress on private associations as a key to American democracy is echoed in Mori's fascination with YMCA and other religious, educational, and philanthropic organizations that abound in the United States.

Is there anything uniquely "Japanese" about Mori's observations? The reader should be the judge. In comparing his work with earlier European writings, it should be kept in mind that *Life and Resources in America* was one of the first foreign accounts of the United States after the Civil War. The nation was rapidly transforming itself, in the process redefining its identity. Whether or not he actually visited the South, the Midwest, and other parts of the country that he describes, here is a very vivid portrayal of a people forging ahead with productive activities now that the great war has been concluded. "Reconstruction" (although the term is not used) may have reminded him of the "restoration" in the name of which his compatriots back home were trying to transform their society. As a major embassy of high Japanese officials was about to visit the United States (the "Iwakura mission" of 1872), Mori must have thought that the visitors would find much here that they would want to incorporate in undertaking domestic reconstruction.

At one point in the book, Mori notes, "Where men think that they know everything, and boast of their superior wisdom, the presumption is that they have yet much to learn." That statement, one of the rare instances in which he seems to speak his mind, may be said to serve as the guiding principle behind the writing of the book, and so, even today's readers, whether in the United States, in Japan, or elsewhere, who may think they already know so much about the subject, will find much of value in *Life and Resources in America*.

Akira Iriye

NOTES

1. Oscar Handlin and Lilian Handlin, eds., *From the Outer World* (Cambridge: Harvard University Press, 1996).

2. Peter Duus, ed., *The Japanese Discovery of America* (Boston: Bedford Books, 1997).

3. Kafu Nagai, *American Stories*, Mitsuko Iriye, trans. (New York: Columbia University Press, 2000).

Acknowledgments

For their help and advice at various stages of this project, which has taken longer than expected (Isn't that always the case?), I would like to thank the following people: Edward R. Beauchamp, Rebekka Brooks, Roger Daniels, Hedi Hong, Akira Iriye, Glenn A. May, Andre Millard, Shelia Smith and Yone Sugita.

John E. Van Sant
Birmingham, Alabama
May 2003

Introduction

East Meets West: Mori Arinori and the Formative Years of United States–Japan Relations

Knowledge shall be sought throughout the world so as to strengthen the foundations of imperial rule.

Emperor Meiji, April 6, 1868

When United States Navy Commodore Matthew C. Perry and his fearsome "black ships" appeared in Uraga Bay, just off the coast of Edo in July 1853, Japan's government leaders—the Tokugawa *bakufu*—were forced to deal with a genuine threat from the West.[1] At the start of the Tokugawa era in the early seventeenth century, Japan had massive and powerful samurai armies that brushed off the then-major Western powers of Spain and Portugal, and forced Dutch merchants to live and work on a small, heavily guarded island in Nagasaki Bay. By the mid-nineteenth century, however, Japan was no longer an economic or military match for even a middling power such as the United States. The long Tokugawa era (1600–1868) advanced Japan's already impressive cultural and artistic achievements. It also witnessed the development of a sophisticated urban society (especially in Edo, Osaka, and Kyoto), a national transportation network of roads, and a commercial economy with a rising merchant class. And a handful of Japanese "Dutch studies" scholars contributed to Japan's scientific knowledge, especially in the area of medicine.

Nevertheless, by the nineteenth century the Tokugawa *bakufu* was constantly confronted by serious internal problems affecting all four major hereditary classes of Japanese society: samurai, farmers, artisans, and merchants.[2] As the economy expanded and became increasingly commercialized, many merchants became wealthy. Many samurai—the elite of Japanese society— became poorer, largely because stipends allotted to them by their *daimyō* (domain lords) did not rise along with higher prices in the increasingly commercialized economy. In fact, their stipends were often reduced, and some samurai were released from service altogether because their *daimyō* could no longer afford to keep them. These *rōnin*, or "masterless" samurai, were more destitute and depressed than the literary myths of *rōnin* as swashbuckling heroes and villains. Many farmers were distressed by the rice tax they had to constantly pay (usually 50 percent of their harvest) to the samurai who, in the opinion of farmers, contributed nothing in return. Prolonged famines in the 1830s led to an upsurge in rebellions against *daimyō* and Tokugawa authorities, especially Oshio Heiachiro's rebellion in Osaka in 1837. Worse, hundreds of thousands of Japanese died during the 1830s from malnutrition, starvation, disease, and Tokugawa *bakufu* ineptitude in distributing rice to the worst famine-hit regions of the country. In other words, Japanese society was unraveling from within.[3]

At this vulnerable historical moment, the West knocked on Japan's door. Russian, British, and American ships began appearing off Japan's coasts with upsetting frequency. The China trade and North Pacific whaling had drawn most of these ships close to Japan's shores. Japan turned down their occasional requests for trade because it would have violated the centuries-old policy of not allowing contact between Japan and Western countries, except for limited contact allowed with the Dutch.[4] After the Opium War of 1839–1841 between the British and the nearby Middle Kingdom of China, it became obvious to foresighted Japanese that someday the increasingly powerful and arrogant Westerners were not going to take Japan's "no" for a definitive answer to their requests for trade and contact. Western requests would soon become demands. More than two centuries of external peace resulted in deteriorated military strength in Japan, and large-scale industrialization had yet to begin. When the United States decided to make a determined effort to "open" Japan to the West by sending Commodore Perry and his black ships in 1853–1854, Japan had no choice but to comply.[5]

The Tokugawa government reluctantly signed treaties on trade, extraterritoriality, and other matters with the United States, Russia, Britain, Holland, and France during the 1850s. Perry's intrusion and these "unequal treaties" (formally known as the Ansei treaties) opened up a Pandora's box of long-simmering internal grievances in Japan. For fifteen years following Perry's expedition, motley bands of anti-Tokugawa and antiforeign samurai waged campaigns of intrigue, assassination, and sometimes war under the rallying cry of "revere the emperor, expel the barbarian." Then the large domains and previous mutual enemies of Satsuma and Choshu joined together and rallied the divided *tōbaku* (antibakufu) forces together, and overthrew the Tokugawa *bakufu* in early 1868. Tokugawa Yoshinobu, the last shogun, resigned and returned to his home domain. Although battles continued to rage in northern Japan for more than a year, it was clear that 268 years of Tokugawa rule was over.[6] A new government, led mostly by the triumphant samurai from Satsuma and Choshu, was founded in the name of a new imperial sovereign, the sixteen-year-old Emperor Meiji.[7]

Meanwhile, the Mexican-American War (1846–1848) resulted in the conquest of vast Southwest and Pacific territories, including California. As soon as the war was over, news spread that gold had been discovered in California, inciting an international rush to the country's newest Pacific territory. The late 1840s was the high point of Manifest Destiny: the political, moral, divinely ordained, and self-righteous philosophy of territorial and commercial expansion on the American continent. The acquisition of Southwest and Pacific territories expanded the United States into a continent-wide empire, and Commodore Perry's expedition to Japan was a forward projection of this expansionist impulse. However, Manifest Destiny and the acquisition of new territories also exacerbated the sectional controversy between northern and southern states over the expansion of slavery. Throughout the 1850s, there were constant political battles and short-lived compromises over the issue of extending slavery to new territories and new states. In 1861, these political battles and failed compromises erupted into the American Civil War—the deadliest war in American history.

Immediately after the war, the federal government embarked on a massive program of reconstruction to renovate the nation's political, economic, and social institutions. It abolished slavery, conferred the right to vote on newly freed black men, rebuilt much of the infrastructure destroyed during the war, and established a public education system in the South. Unfortunately, the reconstruction program was also plagued by scandals, controversy, and entrenched racism. Southern whites were especially upset at the continued presence of federal troops. Most significantly, Reconstruction clearly failed to transform the economic and social relations of the antebellum South.

After Perry's expedition was completed in 1854, American officials in Washington, D.C., paid relatively little attention to Japan because the crises over slavery, the Civil War, and Reconstruction diverted their attention from most foreign relations issues. On the other hand, Japanese officials paid more attention to the United States than to any other foreign country from the 1850s to the 1870s. After all, it was a United States Navy officer who "opened" Japan to the West and American minister (ambassador) Townsend Harris who negotiated the first comprehensive diplomatic treaties between Japan and the West. In 1860, the Tokugawa shogun sent a large delegation of high-ranking officials to ratify treaties between the two countries and meet with American officials, including President James Buchanan.[8] In 1871, the new Meiji government sent an even larger and higher-ranking delegation of officials to the United States and Europe led by an imperial prince, Iwakura Tomomi.[9] To prepare for the Iwakura embassy during its stay in Washington, D.C., the Meiji government sent its first resident diplomat to the United States, a young man who had lived for a few years overseas and excelled at Western studies.

MORI ARINORI'S WESTERN EDUCATION

Mori Arinori (1847–1889) was born and raised in Satsuma during this mid-nineteenth-century era of internal and external strife and transformation in Japan.[10] From a relatively high-ranking samurai family, Mori quickly demonstrated a strong aptitude for education and was sent to the Zoshikan—the Satsuma domain academy for samurai from high-ranking families—and then on to the Kaiseijo, an academy devoted to Western studies established by Satsuma's *daimyō*, Shimazu Nariakira. Earlier than probably any other *daimyō* —and before Perry's intrusion into Japan—Shimazu realized that the barbarians from the West had significantly altered Japan's place in the world. Furthermore, Shimazu realized that if Satsuma could learn and utilize Western science and technology, the domain might be able to oust their Tokugawa overlords. He encouraged Satsuma's samurai to learn Western science and technology, and young Mori was one of those who excelled at these studies. In 1865, Mori was one of nineteen samurai students secretly dispatched (i.e., without the knowledge or permission of the Tokugawa government) by the Satsuma *daimyō* to England to expand their knowledge of the West.[11] Most of these students took courses at the University College of London for more than one year and spent some time traveling on the European continent. Mori spent some of his time in St. Petersburg, where he learned of Orthodox Christianity and of Peter the Great, who had transformed Russia more than 100 years earlier by adopting reforms based on Western methods. By the spring of 1867, the lack of money was becoming a major problem for these Japanese students because Satsuma was concentrating all of its resources on the intensifying battle against the Tokugawa government. Most decided to return home. However, six journeyed to the United States to join the Brotherhood of the New Life, a quasi-Christian and utopian colony at Brocton in upstate New York.[12]

Lawrence Oliphant, mentor and sponsor of the Japanese students, and formerly a member of the British legation in Edo; and Thomas Lake Harris, the leader of the Brotherhood of the New Life, on a visit to England in the spring of 1867, offered free passage, room, board, and education to any of the Satsuma students who would go and live at the colony in New York.

Mori was one of six who accepted the offer.[13] Five more young Japanese men, all from Satsuma, made their way to the Brotherhood of the New Life at Brocton by November 1867—this was the largest group of Japanese living in the United States at the time.

The Brotherhood of the New Life was one of a number of utopian communities that flourished during the nineteenth century, as did reform movements and "new" religions in Europe and the United States. The nineteenth century was an era of dramatic social and economic transformations around the world, especially those caused by the political and industrial revolutions that began a century earlier. For many people, the nineteenth century was an uncertain, unstable, alienating age, and they sought to find personal meaning through religion, by participating in a reform movement (such as anti-slavery), or even by joining a utopian community in the quest for a peaceful environment that would be safe from the dramatic and unsettling changes taking place all around them. Many of these utopian communities were religious, where a spiritual quest of Christian love and devotion was the process to attain a peaceful, even "perfect" life of complete harmony.

It is doubtful that the six Japanese who agreed to go to New York and join the Brotherhood of the New Life community clearly understood Thomas Lake Harris's theology, a theology loosely based upon the ideas and visions of Emanuel Swedenborg. They were impressed (and made impressionable) by Harris's mystically charismatic persona. And their studies of Western science had expanded into the realm of Western cultural values, values which were still new to the young Japanese samurai. Furthermore, Mori and the others were young and eager to explore and learn of the United States—then a Western country on the rise. Thomas Lake Harris was literally their ticket to do just that.

Mori remained with the Brotherhood of the New Life colony in the United States until June 1868 when he and Sameshima Naonobu decided to return to their homeland in the wake of Satsuma's leading role in toppling the Tokugawa government. At this point we get a glimpse of Mori's personal beliefs in Christianity from a letter he and Sameshima composed as they were leaving the Brotherhood of the New Life: "We still feel, yea more and more, inexpressibly grateful towards the Lord one Heavenly Father, for He is through his beloved servant T. L. Harris working so infinitely and so mercifully for the salvation of all inhabitants on the globe."[14]

Soon after his return to Japan, Mori joined the new Satsuma-Choshu dominated Meiji government in Tokyo and worked primarily on diplomatic and military affairs. In July 1869, he submitted a proposal to the deliberative assembly (the *Kōgisho*) that called for all samurai, with the exception of government officials, to relinquish their swords. The sword was a prime symbol of the samurai, the elite warrior-protectors of Japan, and Mori's proposal was seen as an attack on this glorious (and often exaggerated) samurai tradition. Mori's proposal was unanimously voted down, and he was forced to resign from the government for having the audacity to submit such a proposal. Mori returned to Satsuma and started a school for teaching Western languages, especially English. Mori was ahead of his time. Three years later, the Meiji government adopted a more sweeping sword-abolition law.

THE CHARGÉ D' AFFAIRES

In October 1870, Foreign Minister Sawa Nobuyoshi recalled Mori to government service and appointed him as the chargé d' affaires of the new Japanese legation in Washington, D.C.[15] With this appointment, Mori became Japan's first resident diplomat in the United States capital. Mori's fluency in English, his firsthand knowledge of the West and the United States, and his pedigree as a high-status samurai from Satsuma were strong factors in his appointment despite his youth—he was only twenty-three years old—and his faux pas with the sword-abolition proposal. He arrived in Washington to take up his duties in late February 1871, where he remained until March 1873.[16]

Despite his Western studies and overseas experiences, Mori did not have much practical background knowledge in the conduct of state-to-state diplomatic relations. Indeed, very few Japanese had any such practical experience at the beginning of the Meiji era. Mori often relied upon the advice and counsel of Hamilton Fish, the United States secretary of state. He also relied on Charles Lanman, the American secretary whom he hired in the spring of 1871, and Joseph Henry, prominent scientist and first director of the Smithsonian Institution for advice.

The major reason Mori was dispatched by the Japanese government to Washington, D.C., was to prepare for and assist the Iwakura embassy, which stayed in Washington from February 29 to July 27, 1872. Led by Prince Iwakura Tomomi, this embassy included many of the Meiji government's top officials, including Okubo Toshimichi, Ito Hirobumi, and Kido Takayoshi (Koin), along with many lower-level officials and assistants. Starting in the United States, the Iwakura embassy then traveled to several European countries. The political objective of this diplomatic mission was to renegotiate the "unequal treaties" between Japan and several Western countries signed in the wake of Perry's mission of 1853–1854. Unfortunately for Japan, the United States and all European countries refused to renegotiate the treaties during the Iwakura embassy, primarily because they felt that Japan's legal system did not yet measure up to "Western" standards. A second objective for this

Japanese embassy was to study the West. Japanese officials carefully observed American and European science, business methods, educational systems, government systems, and many other aspects of Western society and culture during the nearly two-year duration of the Iwakura embassy. They also brought fifty-eight Japanese students to study at American and European educational institutions, and several American and European teachers and scientists were hired to work in Japan as *yatoi* ("foreign experts") for one or two years.[17] Despite the failure to renegotiate the "unequal treaties," much of the "intellectual technology" acquired during the Iwakura embassy of 1871–1872 was both directly and indirectly utilized in Japan and significantly contributed to the country's industrialization in the second half of the nineteenth century.

Mori arranged meetings between Japanese officials with their American counterparts; he arranged visits to nearby schools, factories, military bases, prisons, and libraries; and he was often included in meetings as both an interpreter and participant. In the official record of the Iwakura mission, however, he is barely mentioned.[18] According to Kido Takayoshi's diary, Mori and the secretaries of Japan's Washington legation were too willing to openly criticize Japan and Japanese society in conversations with Americans. Mori also had the exasperating habit of disagreeing with Kido, Iwakura, and other Japanese officials.[19] To these older and higher-ranking officials, Mori was technically skilled at organizational matters and had an excellent command of English. But he was young, naively enamored of Western and American ways, and did not understand the importance and dignity of Japanese traditions. According to Kido's diary, at one point Prince Iwakura "reproached Mori for his continuing lack of patriotism."[20]

Including the students brought by the Iwakura embassy, Mori's duties as the chargé d' affaires included maintaining watch over approximately 200 Japanese students (high school and college) then in the United States. He also produced three, mostly English-language works during his two years in Washington: *Life and Resources in America*, a book first published in late 1871; "Religious Freedom in Japan," an essay completed in November 1872; and *Education in Japan: A Series of Letters Addressed by Prominent Americans to Arinori Mori*, published in January 1873. The first two of these works are included in this 2004 edition.[21]

LIFE AND RESOURCES IN AMERICA

Life and Resources in America is the most extensive of these works, both in quantity and in its diversity of social, political, and cultural topics. The first edition was published in late 1871 and then republished with no changes in the fall of 1872 as part III of Lanman and Mori's *The Japanese in America*.[22] *The Japanese in America* was republished, with some additional descriptive material, as *Leaders of the Meiji Restoration in America* in 1931.[23] *Life and Resources in America* has been recently republished in Japan within a compilation of Mori's writings, *Shinshu Mori Arinori Zenshu* [A New Collection of Writings by Mori Arinori].[24] For most people, the only way to obtain one of these editions is with access to a university interlibrary loan service. Therefore, a major purpose for the publication of this new edition of *Life and Resources in America* is to make this little-known, yet intriguing, document on American social, cultural, and political life available and affordable to any scholar, student, or interested layperson.

Two issues need to be acknowledged and briefly discussed, or problematized, as some of my colleagues would put it. First is the issue of authorship. On the title page of the first edition of *Life and Resources in America*, published in 1871, is stated: "Prepared under the Direction of Arinori Mori. For circulation in Japan." The preface to *The Japanese in America*, published in 1872, states that *Life and Resources in America* was "compiled under the direction of Jugoi Arinori Mori, the Chargé d'Affaires from Japan" (*jugoi* is "fifth court rank, junior grade"). Charles Lanman later wrote that Mori "caused the publication, for the benefit of his countrymen, of a work on the *Resources of America* [*sic*]."[25] These statements indicate that Mori Arinori did not single-handedly and single-mindedly write this work. Lanman, who worked part-time at the legation and was formerly a librarian with the House of Representatives, did much of the research and wrote many of the draft chapters on subjects chosen by Mori. Mori edited Lanman's original drafts, primarily by adding his personal observations and analyses.[26] As Ivan Hall writes, "although Lanman's in point of research and expression, [*Life and Resources in America*] was Mori's in overall concept, with his editorial hand clearly visible on points of judgement."[27] According to today's book publishing standards, the cover should probably read: "*Life and Resources in America*, by Mori Arinori, with Charles Lanman." To make the issue of authorship even more complicated, as soon as he took up his post as Japan's chargé d'affaires in late February 1871, Mori informed Japanese students studying in the United States that they were to send him short essays on social and cultural subjects of their own choosing.[28] Mori almost certainly utilized some of the information and ideas from these student essays when he edited and revised Lanman's draft chapters.

It should not be surprising, however, that *Life and Resources in America* is actually a composite work. Many books encompassing a wide swath of social, cultural, and political territory are not wholly conceived, researched, composed, and edited by a single individual. For example, there was a Frenchman who wrote a somewhat famous book on the social, cultural, and political landscape of the United States based upon his nine-month trip to America in 1830. He was accompanied by Gustave de Beaumont on this journey, and then had three research assistants help him write both volumes of his magnum opus.[29] "*Democracy in America* is the work of a genius," write Harvey Mansfield and Debra Winthrop in their introduction to the latest edition of Alexis de Tocqueville's eloquent and perceptive classic, "but it was not produced in solitary isolation."[30]

Life and Resources in America was also "not produced in solitary isolation." Yet, we can regard Mori Arinori as the primary author because he conceived and directed this project of compiling information and observations of American social, cultural, and political life. He made substantial contributions based upon his personal knowledge and experiences of the United States and Europe. All evidence of Mori's English language ability indicates that he was extremely good at both speaking and writing English and, therefore, it is safe to assume that he could make substantial contributions to a work that was composed and published in English.[31] Furthermore, the liberal, individualist views expressed in *Life and Resources in America* are similar to the views Mori expressed in the journal *Meiroku Zasshi*, which he helped to establish soon after returning to Japan from his post in Washington.[32]

The other problematic issue is that *Life and Resources in America* was not published in the Japanese language. Both the 1871 and 1872 editions state that *Life and Resources in America* was intended to be published in Japanese, and it's clear from the text that it was intended for a Japanese audience. Yet there is no surviving evidence that it was ever translated and published in Japanese. Mori did send copies of the 1871 edition to government officials in Tokyo just before the Iwakura embassy departed from Japan so they would have some knowledge of the political, social, and cultural life of the United States before they arrived. Indeed, it appears that Mori was primarily addressing the work to them. Many of these officials had some ability in English, and most government departments did have one or more translators. Therefore, it is safe to assume that *Life and Resources in America* helped inform the Japanese government about Americans and the United States.

Why did Mori not follow through and have *Life and Resources in America* published in Japanese? During the first few years of the Meiji era, the new government was still consolidating and legitimizing itself in the face of lingering discontent from Tokugawa supporters. There were also officials within the Meiji government who were less than enthusiastic about the government's growing relationship with the barbarian West. Saigo Takamori, the influential military commander from Satsuma who routed Tokugawa forces in Edo in early 1868 and became one of the most important members of the new Meiji government, left the government he helped create in part because of its "pro-West" policies. In 1876–1877, he led a massive, but failed, rebellion against the Meiji government.[33] Perhaps Mori (or his superiors) decided that a government official should not publish a relatively positive portrayal of the United States in Japan because of still unstable internal political circumstances. It is clear from Kido Takayoshi's diary that some members of the Japanese government felt Mori was too enthusiastic and trusting of American ways. Another possibility is that Mori was constantly writing and constantly busy with government duties most of his life and perhaps never made the time to either translate the work himself or select a publisher for this task. In other words, political circumstances may have precluded publication in Japanese in the early 1870s. Or perhaps there is a more mundane explanation for why *Life and Resources in America* was not published in Japanese. Whatever the reason, only a relative handful of Japanese people could have actually read *Life and Resources in America* at the time, and so the work obviously had limited direct impact with the Japanese public.

Life and Resources in America can be read at least three different, yet interconnected ways. First, it is primarily a descriptive work on the American social, cultural, and political landscape, circa 1870. While commendations and criticisms are apparent in every chapter, most of the work is consciously observational rather than judgmental. As such, it can be read as a document describing American society half a decade after the Civil War. Secondly, it can be read as what a young, educated, male, sometimes pompous, sometimes naive Japanese official observed and believed about the United States. And thirdly, one can read the work for what Mori and Lanman intended, "to introduce American culture to Japan" as Inuzuka Takaaki puts it.[34] Most Japanese knew very little about the United States or the West at this time, but were clearly interested in learning more. For example, after accompanying the shogun's embassy to the United States in 1860, and another delegation to Europe in 1861, Fukuzawa Yukichi published *Things Western (Seiyo Jijo)* in 1867. The book became a runaway best-seller and Fukuzawa became famous throughout Japan—and infamous to the antiforeign diehards who threatened his life.[35]

Less than a century old as a political entity known as the United States, the country was still considered a "new" kind of country, one that had adopted many elements of the eighteenth-century European Enlightenment. It was a country where "the people" were citizens with rights the government was obligated to observe and protect. They were not "subjects" at the constant beck and call of a monarch's wishes, taxes, and wars. The United States adopted and adapted philosophy, technology, and culture from other countries and added original, often utilitarian ideas to build a new country that was politically, economically, demographically, and territorially expanding throughout the nineteenth century.

After the revolution against the old regime of the Tokugawa shogun, Japan saw itself as a "new" country, much like the United States after its own revolution against Britain. While the imperial powers of Britain, France, Russia, Holland, and Germany were seen as old regime countries posing a military threat to Japan, paradoxically the United States was not. The memory of Commodore Perry's gunboat diplomacy of 1853–1854 drifted from that of imminent threat; to a call for violent, revolutionary action against the Tokugawa *bakufu* by a motley group of samurai warriors claiming to "revere the Emperor and expel the barbarian"; and finally to the new Meiji government's trial-and-error policies to create a "new" Japan strong enough to maintain its independence and gain admittance to the community of industrialized, "civilized" nations. To accomplish this long-term task, the Meiji government had immediately adopted the fundamental policy of "rich nation, strong army" *(fukoku kyōhei)*.[36] This policy was designed to create an economy that could compete with the stronger powers of the West in a growing, internationalizing marketplace and pay for a new military force with an army and navy comprised largely of conscripts using modern weapons rather than hereditary samurai and their handsomely crafted, yet outdated, swords.

On a cultural level, Japan's intelligentsia promoted "civilization and enlightenment" *(bunmei kaika)* as Japan's weltanschauung.[37] This was especially true during the first decade of the Meiji era. Mori reflected this spirit in his "Preliminary Note" to *Life and Resources in America*:

> The knowledge furnished by all the better qualified minds of the world is a powerful element, rendering great service in the cause of humanity. It is often the case that enmity and bloodshed are the consequence of storing up prejudice, resulting from the want of mutual knowledge of the parties engaged. The object of this publication is not only to aid in removing those prejudices, but also to invite all the lovers of their race in Japan to join in the noble march of progress and human happiness.

Such a statement of purpose is certainly representative of the *bunmei kaika* spirit of Japan during the 1870s; a progressive, utilitarian spirit that stressed the examination of Western science, methods, and values for possible adaptation in Japan. Mori Arinori was both a government official and a member of the *bunmei kaika* intelligentsia, and in *Life and Resources in America* the reader can observe Mori's interest in the national elements of a modern, industrial society (i.e., the institutions of government, politics, business, military, and education) and the cultural life of the people who lived in this society.

RELIGIOUS FREEDOM IN JAPAN

The religious beliefs of the West, particularly Christianity, were of intense interest and political debate in Japan during the 1860s and 1870s. Japanese had been prohibited from converting to Christianity since the early seventeenth century, and this prohibition was reemphasized soon after the new Meiji government was established in 1868:

> The Christian religion being strictly prohibited by the law of the empire, the violation of this law is considered a serious matter. . . . Care should be taken to induce [Japanese Christians] to renounce their evil ways, and if there be any who refuse to repent, severe punishment must be inflicted.[38]

Some Japanese feared Christianity because the Western powers of the nineteenth century seemed to promote Christianity by sending in missionaries just before sending in their gunboats and troops. In addition, Christianity's highest authority was an unseen, omnipotent divinity; whereas in Japan authority was based upon the secular Five Relationships of Confucianism (ruler–subject, husband–wife, parent–child, older child–younger child, friend–friend). Some feared that if significant numbers of Japanese became Christians, the country would degenerate into social and political anarchy. And Nativists—the hard-core believers in imperial Shinto—argued that Christianity, a foreign religion, would defile the "pure heart" of the Japanese people and was an insult to the Shinto deities who created Japan and protected its purity from time immemorial.[39]

Mori's experience with the Brotherhood of the New Life had given him personal exposure to Christianity, albeit to the unorthodox beliefs of Thomas Lake Harris. He had met with and admired Niijima Jo, a religiously fervent young man who graduated from Amherst College in Massachusetts in 1870 who would go on to establish Doshisha University in Kyoto and become one of Japan's most renowned Christian ministers.[40] In an attempt to minimize the fears, prejudices, and political concerns that many of his fellow Japanese had of the apparent relationship between the Western powers and Christianity, Mori devoted the longest chapter in *Life and Resources in America*, "Religious Life and Institutions," to an overview of Christian beliefs, of churches and denominations, and of the educational and social institutions connected to Christian churches and values. Near the conclusion of this chapter, Mori wrote that,

> According to [my] observations, a very large proportion of the American people are known by the name of Christians, and yet a great many things are

said and done by them, which do not accord with principles of their own Bible. . . . True Christianity may not be considered as identical with the general sense of civilization—in which the good and the bad participate—but true philosophy would seem to teach that it should be a leading element in such civilization.

Criticism of the hypocrisy of some Christians was observant, though not necessarily remarkable. More remarkable was Mori's strong implication that Christianity needed to be a "leading element" in the quest for civilization, primarily because he was a diplomat of a country where conversion to Christianity was against the law.[41]

After *Life and Resources in America* was published and he was still Japan's chargé d' affaires in Washington, D.C., Mori wrote and published "Religious Freedom in Japan," a widely distributed memorial addressed to Prime Minister Sanjo Saneyoshi (Sanetomi) arguing for the repeal of Japan's anti-Christian laws.[42] "In all the enlightened nations of the earth," Mori wrote, "the liberty of conscience, especially in matters of religious faith, is sacredly regarded as not only an inherent right of man, but also as a fundamental element to advance all human interests."[43] But Mori did not stop at advocating religious freedom; he believed it would be to Japan's advantage to adopt Christianity as it's national religion. He argued that, "It is fact, demonstrated by the history of the nations of the earth, among which none have so grandly advanced to the head of civilization as those whose religion has been Christianity."[44] This audacious claim reveals that during his exposure to industrialized Britain and the United States he became convinced of the widespread nineteenth-century Western assumption that there was a connection to Christianity, "progress," and "civilization." Christian nations were civilized nations, and vice versa.

The Japanese government, of course, was not about to adopt Christianity as its national religion no matter how desperately it wanted to enhance the country's strength, independence, and reputation among the Western powers. That was inconceivable. Yet, Japanese officials decided to repeal the laws against Christianity four months after the publication of Mori's memorial on religious freedom. Mori was not single-handedly responsible for this significant change in Japanese law, yet his defense and promotion of Christianity is cited in official publications as being a major reason for the repeal of laws that had been in effect for more than two centuries.[45] This did not lead, as Japanese and foreign missionaries hoped, to a flood of Japanese conversions to Christianity. Nevertheless, the repeal of the anti-Christian edicts removed a major bone of contention between Japan and the West during Japan's journey to become a major industrialized nation.

POST-AMERICA

After he returned to Japan in 1873, Mori and Fukuzawa Yukichi cofounded *Meirokusha* (Meiji 6 Society), a group of Japanese intelligentsia who advocated the adoption of Western liberalism during the *bunmei kaika* era of the 1870s.[46] Mori also cofounded the Commercial Training School in Tokyo, which later evolved into Hitotsubashi University, one of Japan's major universities to this day. He would go on to serve the Foreign Ministry in diplomatic posts in China (1875–1878) and Britain (1879–1884), and in 1885 he became the education minister.

Mori's liberalism of the *bunmei kaika* era gave way to Japan's increasing sense of state nationalism in the 1880s. As education minister, he instituted policies which demanded that schools, teachers, principals, and students at all levels become mentally and physically disciplined and devoted servants of the nation and emperor. Education was for the purpose of serving the nation, not for serving the individual. *Kuni no tame ni* ("for the sake of the nation") had become the essence of government policies, and Mori strongly supported such policies. Yet, Mori's growing nationalism was secular and did not include the quasi-mystical belief in imperial Shinto as the primary element in Japan's political order. He strongly objected to the heavy infusion of Confucian ideology with Shinto worship promoted by other government officials, including his colleagues in the Education Ministry. He had consistently believed that religious beliefs were an individual matter, and should not be promoted or hindered by the government.

On the morning of February 11, 1889, Mori dressed in his finest Western formal clothes at his ministerial residence in Nagata-cho. Later that day, the emperor would announce the promulgation of the Meiji Constitution and all cabinet ministers, top government officials, and foreign ambassadors were scheduled to be in attendance at the Imperial Palace for this symbolic event signifying the arrival of "Modern" Japan. Just before he was about to depart, Mori agreed to see a young man dressed in kimono who had told Mori's steward that he needed to personally report an important matter to the education minister. As soon as the young man started to speak to Mori, he pulled a knife out of his kimono sleeve and thrust it deep into Mori's abdomen twice before Mori's bodyguard grabbed his sword and killed the attacker with two swift blows. Despite the quick action of the bodyguard, Mori's wounds were fatal. He soon lost consciousness and died early the next morning.

The attacker had a "manifesto" in a pocket inside his kimono which revealed his name as Nishino Buntaro. The manifesto claimed that the education minister had shown disrespect to the Shinto gods at the Grand Shrines of Ise during a visit more than a year earlier and Nishino was avenging this blasphemy. Mori's tragic death was not the first time, nor would it be the last, that a top Japanese official was assassinated for allegedly disrespecting the gods or thwarting the imperial will.

INTERPRETING MORI
AND HIS SIGNIFICANCE TO MEIJI JAPAN

This introduction has emphasized Mori Arinori's early career because *Life and Resources in America* and "Religious Freedom in Japan" were produced during this early stage of Mori's professional life and intellectual thought. At this point, let us step back and attempt an interpretation of Mori's life and significance to the Meiji era as a whole. What were his contributions? What should we remember of his role during this transformative era of Japanese history?

He left behind a substantial paper trail of documents, letters, and other writings that scholars such as Ivan Parker Hall, Hayashi Takeji, Okubo Toshiaki, and Alistair Swale have thoroughly mined. But Mori remains enigmatic and difficult for scholars to interpret because, like most people, his thinking changed, meandered, and evolved as he grew older and gained more experience both at home and abroad. He also divided his time between thinking and writing about social, political, and cultural issues, especially during the first decade of the Meiji era and early in his adult life; and being a government servant who devised, negotiated, and implemented policies to internally strengthen the country and to externally enhance his country's reputation during the later years of his life.

We can, on a general level, interpret Mori as being part of the *bunmei kaika* movement of the 1870s. He promoted the adoption and adaptation of those elements from the West that he believed would prove useful to a modernizing Japanese society. He believed that government was meant to serve the people, and individuals should be allowed to believe whatever they wanted to and worship whatever deities met their spiritual needs. Essentially, people should be allowed to pursue life, liberty, and happiness as long as they didn't threaten the stability of the state. He even criticized Japanese ways in discussions with Americans when the Iwakura embassy was in Washington negotiating for more international respect for Japan. And he clearly went too far in his naive proposal to abolish the Japanese written language in favor of English because it was more utilitarian. In many respects, he reflected the ideals of eighteenth-century Enlightenment thought. His writings, while serving in Washington and as a member of *Meirokusha,* clearly reflect this liberal, even idealist, phase of his career and thinking.

Yet, Mori was not of the stature of Fukuzawa Yukichi or Nishi Amane or other intellectuals whom we associate with *bunmei kaika*. Nor did he support the People's Rights Movement as it gained steam in the late 1870s. This movement, led by ex-samurai who felt they had been shut out of the best government positions by the Satsuma and Choshu leaders of the new Meiji government, wanted a more direct, representative voice in government policies. Mori, a Satsuma man, probably did not relish the thought of including a substantial number of "outsiders" in top government positions. And he did not advocate "the people" having direct influence on government policies. He had seen in nineteenth-century America how "direct" democracy led to a spoils system where unqualified, incompetent, and uncultured people received government appointments simply because they supported a winning candidate for elective office. Individual liberties and rights were all well and good, but unqualified people of questionable character should not be running the government.

Later in life, during his time as the Japanese minister to London and as education minister, Mori came to reflect the *kuni no tame ni* spirit of the latter half of the Meiji era, as superbly discussed and analyzed by Carol Gluck and Takashi Fujitani.[47] Perhaps to compensate for the lingering suspicions that he was a slavish promoter of all things Western and Christian, Mori emphasized duty and devotion to country and emperor. Education was primarily for the purpose of serving national interests, and secondarily individual interests. Students and teachers had to be morally, intellectually, and physically trained and ready to serve the nation whenever called upon to do so. The nation-serving policies designed and adopted during his tenure as education minister (1885–1889) evolved into a regimented system that remained in force until the end of World War II. The constitutional monarchy systems of Britain, and especially Germany, appealed to him. Though he did not play a major role in drafting the Meiji Constitution, he supported Ito Hirobumi's ultimately successful effort at designing a constitution where people had limited rights, and were to consider themselves as "subjects" of nation and emperor.

One might say that Mori joined the conservative, nationalist bandwagon as did so many others in Japan in the 1880s. Then again, much of the world had become more nationalist in the nineteenth century; Japan and Mori were just catching up. Symbolic of Mori's apparent shift from liberalism to conservative nationalism are his two wedding ceremonies. In 1875, he married Hirose Tsuneko in a highly publicized, Western-style civil ceremony followed by a lavish reception that dazzled all of Tokyo. After divorcing in 1886, Mori married Iwakura Hiroko in 1887, a daughter of Prince Iwakura Tomomi, whom Mori had always respected but in the 1870s thought of as emblematic of the Old Japan. And his 1887 wedding ceremony was a low-key, Japanese-style affair.

As noted earlier, Mori, the education minister, objected to the heavy infusion of neo-Confucianism and Shinto mythology as part of the morals education for students and teachers. Since the early 1870s, he consistently believed that religious beliefs were individual rights and not to be encouraged or enforced or limited by the state. Nor is there any indication that he believed the imperial family to be descended from the Shinto gods. The *Imperial Rescript on Education*, that quintessential document of Japan's regimented education system and emperor worship, was written and issued more than a year after Mori's death. He had no connection to this infamous declaration of Japan's national myth.

We can recall two fundamental, historical memories of Mori: the young, liberal Westernizer of the 1870s; and the mature nationalist and statist of the 1880s. In his comprehensive and complex biography, Ivan Parker Hall locates four "images" of Mori: the commendable Westernizer; the reckless, reprehensible Westernizer; the commendable nationalist; and the reprehensible nationalist and imperialist.[48] When one tries to imagine Mori on the political, ideological, and intellectual spectrums of historical memory, chronology is important because Mori's views, like those of many people, shift over time. Furthermore, Mori was both an intellectual and a government official. It would be unfair to say that these positions are incompatible, but clearly such occupations conflict as much as they complement one another. To problematize even more, Mori died at the relatively young age of forty-one. At the risk of delving into hypothetical history, he certainly would have contributed more in either or both areas of intellectual thought and government service had he lived another two or three decades.

By the time Emperor Meiji died in 1912, Japan had machine-based industries, a capitalist economy, a systematic government and legal system, and a public education system. Japan defeated China (in 1895) and Russia (in 1905) in major wars, and gained its first colonial territories in Taiwan and Korea. Japan was the only country outside of Europe and the United States that successfully industrialized, albeit at tremendous personal cost to many Japanese themselves. Some elements of proto-industrialization were in existence during the Tokugawa Era; but it was the challenge from the West beginning in the mid-nineteenth century that convinced Japan's leaders that the only way their country would survive meant adopting and adapting the sciences, governing institutions, and economic systems of the West to Japan's own traditions. There was no secret formula for combining the methods and practices of the West to the traditions and culture of Japan. The Meiji era was often a period of trial and error, especially in the early years. Japan had gone through previous eras of adopting and adapting systems, practices, even beliefs (Buddhism and Confucianism, for example) from the outside and ultimately internalizing these as part of their own traditional culture. Despite exaggerated notions of being a "closed country," Japan has historically had a transcultural or transnational approach to learning. Before the nineteenth century, Japan usually looked to the Asian continent with *Wakon, Kansai* or "Japanese spirit, Chinese learning." From the mid-nineteenth century, Japan's gaze shifted to *Wakon, Yosai*, or "Japanese spirit, Western learning."

Mori Arinori was not among the most influential political leaders of the Meiji era. Yet, he was a significant government official who contributed to Japan's conduct of foreign affairs and the formation of education policies. Likewise, he is not remembered among the first rank of Meiji era intelligentsia. Nevertheless, he certainly contributed to early Meiji intellectual discourse, particularly during the heady days of *bunmei kaika*. As one of the first overseas students, as a member of the intelligentsia, and as a government official, Mori constantly and actively made an effort to improve and strengthen Japan both internally and externally. His writings on America were part of that effort.

A NOTE ON THE TEXT

The following edition of *Life and Resources in America* has been retyped and reformatted from part III of the 1872 edition of Lanman and Mori's *The Japanese in America*. The 1872 edition of *Life and Resources in America* is an exact reproduction of the original 1871 edition, except it was reformatted to fit more words on fewer pages. For anyone who may be interested, there is a facsimile reprint of the 1871 edition of *Life and Resources in America* in Vol. 6 of Okubo, Kaminuma, Inuzuka, eds., *Shinshu Mori Arinori Zenshu.*

The following edition of *Life and Resources in America* is complete, but is not an exact copy of the 1871 and 1872 editions. I have made some grammatical alterations in order to make this 2004 edition more "user-friendly." Mori and Lanman were sometimes in the habit of composing long paragraphs, with long sentences, with an overdose of colons, semicolons, and commas.[49] I have sometimes broken long paragraphs into shorter ones. Some colons and semicolons have been replaced by commas, or even eliminated in order to break long sentences into shorter ones when this could be done easily and without changing the meaning. On rare occasions, a word or two has been inserted to make a sentence comprehensible and these are indicated by [brackets]. There are a few short deletions of material—usually a few words—deemed inconsequential or redundant, and are indicated by [. . .]. I have also added section titles within chapters, and explanatory footnotes in order to make the content of the text more comprehensible. Nevertheless, in order to maintain as much of the original text as possible, I have taken a minimalist approach to editing the text, and most changes involved punctuation. Even so, I am no Strunk and White and have left much of the questionable and awkward punctuation unchanged.

John E. Van Sant

NOTES

1. Perry's ships were referred to by Japanese at the time as *kurofune,* literally "black ships" as their hulls were dark and two of the four ships spewed dark smoke from coal-fired steam engines. The color black can also symbolize death, as it does in Japan and much of East Asia. The official account of the Perry expedition is Francis L. Hawks, *Narrative of the Expedition of an American Squadron to the China Seas and Japan* (New York: D. Appleton & Company, 1857), which was recently republished as Commodore M. C. Perry, *Narrative of the Expedition to the China Seas and Japan, 1852–1854* (Dover Publications, 2000).

2. There were significant divisions within these classes, and members of the imperial family, the Ainu, and the *burakumin* were considered outside of this class system.

3. There are several excellent articles on nineteenth-century Japan in Marius Jansen, ed., *The Cambridge History of Japan, Volume 5, The Nineteenth Century* (Cambridge: Cambridge University Press, 1989).

4. A series of regulations restricting contact between Japan and Western countries was adopted by the Tokugawa government in the 1630s. These regulations became collectively known as the *sakoku* ("closed country") policy. Documents containing these regulations can be found in David J. Lu, *Japan: A Documentary History*, Vol. 1 (New York: M. E. Sharpe, 1997), 220–23. There is significant debate on how "closed" or "open" Japan was during the Tokugawa era. See Ronald Toby, *State and Diplomacy in Early Modern Japan: Asia in the Development of the Tokugawa Bakufu* (Stanford: Stanford University Press, 1991, 2nd edition); Naohiro Asao, *Sakoku* (Tokyo: Shogakkan, 1975); and Brett Walker, "Reappraising the Sakoku Paradigm," *Journal of Asian History*, Vol. 30, No. 2 (1996). For reaction against the West in the first half of the nineteenth century, see Bob Tadashi Wakabayashi, *Anti-Foreignism and Western Learning in Early Modern Japan* (Cambridge: Harvard University Press, 1986).

5. For earlier contacts between the United States and Japan, see Shunzo Sakamaki, *Japan and the United States, 1790–1853* (Tokyo: Asiatic Society of Japan, 1939; reprint, Wilmington, Delaware: Scholarly Resources, Inc. 1973).

6. W. G. Beasley, *The Meiji Restoration* (Stanford: Stanford University Press, 1972), and Conrad Totman, *The Collapse of the Tokugawa Bakufu, 1862–1868* (Honolulu: University of Hawaii Press, 1980) are major studies of this transformative era, in addition to chapters in *The Cambridge History of Japan, Volume 5, The Nineteenth Century.*

7. Donald Keene, *Emperor of Japan: Meiji and His World, 1852–1912* (New York: Columbia University Press, 2002) is the most comprehensive biography in English of this enormously significant, yet enigmatic historical figure. The emperor's personal

name was Mutsuhito while the era name was Meiji. Since the Meiji era (1868–1912), emperors of Japan are referred to by the era name after their deaths. During their reign, they are usually referred to as "the Emperor" rather than their personal names.

8. Awaji-no-kami Muragaki, *Kokkai Nikki: The Diary of the First Japanese Embassy to the United States*, trans., Helen M. Uno (Tokyo: Foreign Affairs Association of Japan, 1958); Masao Miyoshi, *As We Saw Them: The First Japanese Embassy to the United States* (Berkeley: University of California Press, 1979).

9. Kunitake Kume, comp., *The Iwakura Embassy, 1871–73*, 5 vols., Graham Healy and Chushichi Tzuzuki, eds. (Richmond, Surrey, UK: The Japan Documents, Princeton University Press, 2002).

10. Mori was born in Iso, a village on the outskirts of Kagoshima, the capital of Satsuma domain. There are two biographies of Mori in English: Ivan Parker Hall, *Mori Arinori* (Cambridge: Harvard University Press, 1973), and Alistair Swale, *The Political Thought of Mori Arinori: A Study in Meiji Conservatism* (London: Japan Library, Curzon Press, 2000). Two relatively recent biographies in Japanese are Takaaki Inuzuka, *Mori Arinori* (Tokyo: Yoshikawa Kobunkan, 1986), and Takeji Hayashi, *Mori Arinori* (Tokyo: Chikuma Shobo, 1986).

11. For an account of these students, see Andrew Cobbing, *The Satsuma Students in Britain: Japan's Early Search for the Essence of the West* (London: Japan Library, Curzon Press, 2000). Although it has been cataloged with Arthur Cobbing as the author, *The Satsuma Students In Britain* is actually Cobbing's translation and revision of Takaaki Inuzuka, *Satsumahan Eikoku Ryugakusei* (Tokoyo: Chuo Koronsha, 1974).

12. The most extensive collection of materials on Harris and the Brotherhood of the New Life is Jack T. Ericsom, ed., *Thomas Lake Harris and the Brotherhood of the New Life: Books, Pamphlets, Serials, and Manuscripts* (Glen Rock, New Jersey: Microfilming Corporation of America, 1974). For a study, though dated, see Herbert Schneider and George Lawton, *A Prophet and a Pilgrim* (New York: Columbia University Press, 1942).

13. The others were Matsumura Junzo, Hatakeyama Yoshinari, Yoshida Kiyonari, Sameshima Naonobu, and Nagasawa Kanaye. For the Japanese members of the Brotherhood of the New Life, see Paul Akira Kadota and Terry Earl Jones, *Kanaye Nagasawa: A Biography of a Satsuma Student* (Kagoshima, Japan: Kagoshima Prefectural Junior College, 1990); chapter 3 of Hall, *Mori Arinori*; and chapter 4 of John E. Van Sant, *Pacific Pioneers: Japanese Journeys to America and Hawaii, 1850–1880* (Urbana and Chicago: University of Illinois Press, 2000).

14. Sameshima [Noda] and Mori [Sawai] to Yoshida, et. al., June 17, 1868, Ericsom, ed., *TLH* and *BNL*, Reel 13, #302.

15. *Shobenmushi* was the formal Japanese term for chargé d' affaires. Meanwhile, Sameshima Naonobu, Mori's compatriot from Satsuma and fellow student in London and at the Brotherhood of the New Life colony in New York, was appointed Japan's chargé d' affaires in London, with simultaneous responsibilities in Paris and Berlin. Charles Wolcott Brooks, an American, served as consul general of Japan, part-time, in San Francisco from 1858 to 1873.

16. Japanese officials who served under Mori in Washington were Toyama Masakazu, Takagi Saburo, Nawa Michikazu, Magome Tamesuke, and Yatabe Ryokichi. Mori was replaced in 1873 by Yoshida Kiyonari, a fellow Satsuma student in London and at the Brotherhood of the New Life in New York. After the Brotherhood of the New Life, Yoshida spent a couple years studying at Rutgers College in New Jersey.

17. Five of the Japanese students were young girls and three would eventually graduate from American colleges (two from Vassar College and one from Bryn Mawr). See Barbara Rose, *Tsuda Umeko and Women's Education in Japan* (New Haven: Yale University Press, 1992), and Akiko Kuno, *Unexpected Destinations: The Poignant Story of Japan's First Vassar Graduate* (Tokyo: Kodansha International, 1993).

18. Kume Kunitake, comp., *The Iwakura Embassy 1871–73, Vol. 1, The United States of America*, trans. Martin Colcutt (Richmond, Surrey, UK: The Japan Documents, Curzon Press, 2002).

19. Takayoshi Kido, *The Diary of Kido Takayoshi*, Vol. 1, trans. Sidney D. Brown and Akiko Hirota (Tokyo: University of Tokyo Press, 1985), 142, 147, 154, 167, and 181.

20. Ibid., 154.

21. While *Education in Japan* is an interesting documentary source on what some American educators believed of the role and importance of education in modern societies, it is not included in this 2004 volume. In addition to still existing copies of the original edition, there is a facsimile reprint of *Education in Japan* included in Vol. 5 of Toshiaki Okubo, Hachiro Kaminuma, and Takaaki Inuzuka, eds., *Shinshu Mori Aronori Zenshu* 6 vols. (Tokyo: Bunsendo Shoten, 1999).

22. Arinori Mori, *Life and Resources in America* (Washington, D.C.: n.p., 1871); Charles Lanman and Arinori Mori, *The Japanese in America* (New York: University Publishing Company, 1872). *The Japanese in America* was also published in 1872 in London by Longmans, Green, Reader, and Dyer Publishers.

23. Charles Lanman and Arinori Mori, *Leaders of the Meiji Restoration In America*, Yoshiyuki Okamura, ed. (Tokyo: Hokuseido Press, 1931).

24. *Shinshu Mori Arinori Zenshu*, 6 vols. (Tokyo: Bunsendo Shoten, 1997–1999). *Life and Resources in America* is included in Vol. 6. In an earlier collection of Mori's writings, Toshiaki Okuba, ed., *Mori Arinori Zenshu*, 3 vols. (Tokyo: Seibundo, 1971–1973), only Mori's introduction and chapter 7, "Educational Life and Institutions," of *Life and Resources in America* were included.

25. Charles Lanman, *Leading Men of Japan* (Boston: D. Lothrop and Company, 1883), 136.

26. Inuzuka, *Mori Arinori*, 133.

27. Hall, *Mori Arinori*, 175.

28. A selection of these essays was published as part II of Lanman and Mori's *The Japanese in America*.

29. Alexis de Tocqueville, *Democracy in America*, Harvey Mansfield and Debra Winthrop, eds. (Chicago: University of Chicago Press, 2000), xlii. De Tocqueville also heavily relied upon *The Federalist Papers*, James Kent's *Commentaries on the American Law*, and Joseph Story's *Commentaries on the Constitution of the United States*.

30. Ibid.

31. *The Japanese Legation Copybook* (included in *Shinshu Mori Arinori Zenshu*, Vol. 5) contains several notes and letters written in English by Mori, demonstrating a sometimes pretentious and nearly always formal writing style. Some of these letters are in his own handwriting. Furthermore, there is no evidence that Mori's Japanese assistants at the legation acted as his interpretors or translators, and no evidence that Charles Lanman could communicate in Japanese, whether writing or speaking. Mori even suggested that Japan adopt English as its national language as it was more utilitarian than Chinese or Japanese (See Mori, *Education in Japan*, lvi). He was widely criticized for this suggestion.

32. See William R. Braisted, ed. and trans., *Meiroku Zasshi: Journal of the Japanese Enlightenment* (Cambridge: Harvard University Press, 1976).

33. Saigo also left the government because he wanted to lead an invasion of Korea, which other government officials wisely rejected. Saigo's death in 1877, supposedly by ritual suicide, has become the source of many legends.

34. Inuzuka, *Mori Arinori*, 132.

35. See Yukichi Fukuzawa, *The Autobiography of Yukichi Fukuzawa*, trans. Eiichi Kiyooka (New York: Columbia University Press, 1960), chapters 6 and 9 for descriptions of his journeys to the United States, and chapter 11 on "The Risk of Assassination."

36. For example, see the first three chapters of Richard Samuels, *Rich Nation, Strong Army: National Security and the Technological Transformation of Japan* (Ithaca: Cornell University Press, 1994), and Akira Iriye, "Japan's Drive to Great Power Status," in *The Cambridge History of Japan, Volume 5, The Nineteenth Century.*

37. Fukuzawa Yukichi was the most famous promoter of "civilization and enlightenment." His most significant and representative writings from this era are *Things Western* (Seiyo Jijo, 1867); "The Encouragement of Learning" (*Gakumon no Susume*, 1872); and *An Outline of a Theory of Civilization* (*Bunmeiron no Gairyaku*, 1875).

38. "A Decree of the Mikado's Court, June 8, 1868," Department of State, *Foreign Relations of the United States, 1868-1869* (Washington, D.C.: Government Printing Office, 1870), 771.

39. This "school" of thought was known during the Tokugawa era as *Kokugaku*, "national learning." During the late Tokugawa and early Meiji eras, some of the most activist and violent *kokugaku* believers were from Mito domain and are thus sometimes known as the Mito School.

40. Minoru Watanabe, *Niijima Jo* (Tokyo: Yoshikawa Kobunkan, 1959), 80-81; Arthur S. Hardy, ed., *Life and Letters of Joseph Hardy Neesima* (Boston and New York: Houghton Mifflin and Company, 1891). Niijima Jo was called "Joseph Neesima" by his American friends.

41. On the other hand, in *Democracy in America*, Alexis de Tocqueville's many eloquent pages on religion in the United States do not indicate that he observed such hypocrisy.

42. Arinori Mori, "Religious Freedom in Japan: A Memorial and Draft of Charter" (Washington, D.C.: November 1872), a facsimile reprint in Moriaki Sakamoto, *Mori Arinori no Shiso* (Tokyo: Jiji Tsushinsha, 1969), and *Shinshu Mori Arinori Zenshu*, Vol. 2. Charles Lanman was no longer employed by Mori as of August 1872, and thus it is unlikely that he had anything to do with writing this essay.

43. Mori, "Religious Freedom in Japan," 3.

44. Ibid., 7.

45. In *Japanese Religion* (Tokyo: Kodansha International, 1972), a book published under the direction of the Japanese government's Agency for Cultural Affairs, it states on page 83 that Mori, Nakamura Masanao (Keiu), and the Iwakura mission—which Mori advised while it was in the United States—were responsible for the repeal of the anti-Christian edicts. See also Yoshiya Abe, "From Prohibition to Toleration: Japanese Government Views Regarding Christianity, 1854–1873," *Japanese Journal of Religious Studies*, Vol. 5, Nos. 2–3 (June–September 1978).

46. The Meiroku Society existed in one form or another until the early twentieth century, but the *Meiroku Zasshi* was published only from March 1874 to November 1875.

47. Carol Gluck, *Japan's Modern Myths: Ideology in the Late Meiji Period* (Princeton: Princeton University Press, 1985); and T. Fujitani, *Splendid Monarchy: Power and Pageantry in Modern Japan* (Berkeley and Los Angeles: University of California Press, 1996).

48. Hall, 6–8.

49. This writing style was probably the work of Charles Lanman because Mori's English-language letters in the *Japanese Legation Copybook* and his essay, "Religious Freedom in Japan," which Lanman was not involved with, are relatively free of colons and semicolons.

LIFE AND RESOURCES

IN

AMERICA.

PREPARED UNDER THE DIRECTION

OF

ARINORI MORI.

———

For circulation in Japan.

———

WASHINGTON, D.C.

1871.

Preliminary Note

The knowledge furnished by all the better qualified minds of the world is a powerful element, rendering great service in the cause of humanity. It is often the case that enmity and bloodshed are the consequence of storing up prejudices, resulting from the want of mutual knowledge of the parties engaged. The object of this publication is not only to aid in removing those prejudices, but also to invite all the lovers of their race in Japan to join in the noble march of progress and human happiness.

In view of the fact that many dates are mentioned in this volume, it has been found necessary for the sake of convenience, to adopt the western calendar altogether, and it is hoped that this course will not lead to any embarrassment in the mind of the reader.

Mori Arinori

Washington City [D.C.], U.S.

September 1871
Or, according to the Japanese calendar, the Seventh month of the Fourth year of Meiji

Introduction

By the term America, which appears on the title page of this book, we mean the United States of America.[1] As we are writing for the information of a class of readers who have never visited this country, we propose to speak in as simple and concise a manner as possible. Whatever statements of fact we may make, shall be founded upon the public and other authentic records. In submitting any general observations, we shall endeavor to steer a middle course, and give only such opinions as are held in common by the people of the country. Before proceeding to the main object of this volume, however, we think it necessary to take a brief survey of the area and population of the United States as follows:

The total area of the Republic, which extends from the Atlantic Ocean to the Pacific Ocean, and, excepting Alaska, lies wholly in the temperate zone, is about 3,830,000 square miles—an extent of surface larger than the whole of Europe. It has a coast-line, including shores of bays, sounds, and lakes, of 30,000 miles, of which 2,800 are on the Atlantic, 1,800 on the Pacific, and 2,000 on the Gulf of Mexico. It is traversed from north to south by two great ranges of mountains, called Alleghany and Rocky Mountains. [The country's] rivers are numerous, and among the largest in the world; its lakes contain more than one-half of the fresh water on the globe. Its population, according to the census of 1870, is not far from 39,000,000, which is a considerable advance upon the population hitherto claimed for the Empire of Japan.[2] In the last seventy years, the increase has been about 33,000,000. Of

---

1. The use of the pronoun "we" was probably meant to include the Japanese legation in Washington, D.C., as a whole, which included Mori, three (sometimes four) Japanese assistants, and Charles Lanman.

2. In comparison, the population of Japan in 1872 (just after the Meiji government's first comprehensive census) was 33,111,000.

these inhabitants, it has been estimated that more than two-fifths of them are immigrants, or the descendants of immigrants, from foreign countries. Great Britain and Ireland have contributed most largely to this immigration, and the other countries which have helped to swell the population are as follows . . . in the order of their contribution: Germany, France, Prussia, China, West Indies, Switzerland, Norway and Sweden, Holland, Mexico, Spain, Italy, Belgium, South America, Denmark, Azores, Portugal, Sardinia, Poland, and Russia, whose contribution was less than 2,000. Of this great mass of immigrants, it has been ascertained that a very large proportion have changed their circumstances for the better. With regard to the black race, who prior to the year 1860 were in a state of bondage, but are now free, they number nearly 4,900,000. The half-civilized Indian tribes [number] about 26,000, and the wild Indians have been estimated at 300,000. In 1870 there were of Chinese 63,254, with whom were included 53 Japanese, but since then the latter have reached 250 in number.[3]

The public lands of the United States are so abundant, that every man who settles in the country can afford, with careful management, to have a small farm for his exclusive benefit [because] the price of land is generally so reasonable that it scarcely exceeds, and seldom equals, the rent payable in England. There is no description of produce, European or tropical, which may not be raised in the United States; and aside from its many other advantages, there is no other country which offers so many inducements to people in search of permanent and comfortable homes. It is the present condition of the people who enjoy this inheritance, with their manners and customs, that we propose to describe in the following pages of this volume.

But, before concluding this introduction, it is important that two subjects should be mentioned for the special consideration of the Japanese people. While we entertain an exalted opinion of what is called a Republican form of government, we confess that it is not without its disadvantages and dangers. For any foreign nation fully to understand them must require time and much careful study. The Japanese people have been somewhat fascinated by what they have seen of the American government and institutions, and it is of the utmost importance that they should well consider the subject in all its bearings before adopting any of its features into their own form of government. The evils resulting from the misuse of freedom in America are among the most difficult to correct or reform, and ought to be carefully avoided. Another fact that should not be forgotten has reference to the educational qualifica-

---

3. The 1870 United States census was the first to include Japanese, though there had been a few Japanese in the country earlier. Most of the additional 250 Japanese in the United States cited by Mori were students, businessmen, and government officials who had entered the country after the census had been taken in June and July of 1870.

tions necessary to secure success in a Republican form of government. It is undoubtedly true that the best thinkers in America deplore the fact that the machinations of the politicians have resulted in placing the United States in an unfortunate condition in this respect. It has been so profitable with designing and selfish men to increase the number of voters, that they have secured the passage of laws which allow all men to vote, in view of the single idea of personal freedom.[4] This is undoubtedly all wrong, and the evil effects of this state of things are being manifested every day. A prosperous, happy, and permanent Republican government can only be secured, when the people who live under it are virtuous and well educated.

---

4. Mori is probably referring to the Fifteenth Amendment to the United States Constitution, passed in the aftermath of the American Civil War. The amendment gave voting rights to newly freed African American men. Most Southern whites were opposed to voting rights for former slaves, and the issue was controversial among Northern whites as well. Despite this opposition, the Fifteenth Amendment was approved and became effective in 1870.

Chapter One

Official and Political Life

As preliminary to this chapter, it would seem to be necessary that we should give an outline of the machinery of the American Government. It is twofold in its character. First, *Federal*, because it is made up of States, and second, *National*, because it acts directly from the people. According to the Constitution, it is divided into three branches: Executive, Legislative, and Judicial.

The head of the Executive branch, or governor of the nation, is called the President, who is elected by the votes of the people for the term of four years, and is sometimes re-elected for an additional term of four years. He is also the Commander-in-Chief of the United States Navy and Army. The average cost of each election, in money, has been estimated at two millions of dollars [circa 1870], and these expenses are incurred in part by the Government and people. His office is styled the Executive Mansion, [and] is identical with his official residence, the White House. He is obliged to be a native and citizen of the country, and thirty-five years of age. . . . [H]is annual compensation is $25,000. The second officer of the Government is called the Vice-President, whose business is to preside over the Senate. He is elected in the same manner as the President, and his salary is eight thousand dollars per annum. The Executive departments of the Government are seven in number: the departments of State or Foreign Affairs, Treasury, Interior, Post Office, War, Navy, and of Justice. The heads of these are called Secretaries, and they form the Cabinet of the President. They each receive a salary of eight thousand dollars, and their jurisdiction, under the President, extends to all the Subordinate officers of the Government, whether located in Washington or in the several States of the Union.

The Judiciary of the country is vested in a Supreme Court, District Courts, and the Court of Claims. The salaries of the Judges ranging from sixty-five hundred down to $3,500 per annum.[1]

The Legislative branch of the Government consists of a Senate and House of Representatives, two hundred and forty-three, elected for two years, and their compensation is five thousand dollars per annum.

The number of States which form the Union is thirty-seven, with ten Territories or incipient States, and their form of government is precisely similar to that of the nation at large. The leading officers of each State or Territory bearing the titles Governor and Lieutenant-Governor. To the above may be added the municipal form of government for cities and towns where the local authority is allied to that generally recognized in Europe, where the chief officers consist of Mayors and Aldermen and their subordinates, although bearing different names in different countries.

With these particulars before him, the reader will be able to comprehend the following observations. Although the real and official residence of the President is in Washington, the fashionable season . . . begins and ends with the sittings of Congress, beginning in December and lasting three to six months. The position occupied by officials under the Constitution gives them necessarily a certain rank, according to the importance and nature of the office, the length of time, and the age, required by law, of the incumbent. The house in which the President resides is the property of the Government, and, to a great extent, his household expenses are paid by public appropriations. The title by which he is addressed in conversation is that of *Mr. President*, and every citizen of the Republic, no matter how humble his position, has a right to visit the Executive in person. During the winter he holds public receptions as often as once a week, and on the Fourth of July, which is a National Holiday, and the First of January, he receives, as a special mark of respect, the Diplomatic Corps and the officers of the Army and the Navy in full uniform, himself always appearing without any uniform. He accepts no invitations to dinners, and makes no calls or visits of ceremony but is at liberty to visit without ceremony at his pleasure. State dinners are given by him quite frequently, and persons invited commit a breach of etiquette when they decline invitations.

The rules of social intercourse which govern the Cabinet Ministers are similar to those recognized by the President. As their tenure of office is limited, they have . . . a very busy time during their whole term of service; spending their days in dealing out patronage, and their nights in giving or attending par-

---

1. See chapter 13, "Judicial Life," for more detailed information on the judiciary.

ties. Their families take the lead in fashion, and all American citizens have an undisputed right to attend their receptions, and after that public manner, to be fashionable; and as exclusiveness the President or his Ministers would be considered undemocratic, and therefore would not be tolerated, there is no end to the so-called enjoyments of life. If a Minister is rich and liberal, he becomes . . . the biggest man of the hour in spite of his politics. If poor, and dependent only upon his salary, the fact of his having to occupy a large house and to entertain the people invariably sends him into retirement a poorer man than he was before.

With the Judges of the Supreme Court these matters are somewhat different. They are the only dignitaries who hold office for life, and they can afford to do as they please, and generally please to lead the quiet lives of cultivated gentlemen. They go into society when the spirit moves them, are not disinclined to partake of good dinners with their friends, a Foreign Envoy, or a Cabinet Minister; and perhaps the greatest of their blessings is that they are not compelled to curry favor with the multitude.

The next layer of Washington society to which we would allude is made up of the Heads of Bureaus and the Officers of the Army and Navy, their pay ranging from ten to two thousand dollars per annum. They are the men who more immediately manage the machinery of the Government, and upon whom, to a great extent, depends the success of all the public measures enacted by Congress. Though generally well paid, many of them cannot afford to display much style, although they live comfortably and generally in their own houses, although many officials reside in boarding-houses or hotels. The civil officers are but seldom appointed on their merits, but usually through political influence. And the party which happens to be in power commonly claims all the patronage, and the most worthy and competent men are often dismissed from office without a moment's warning. With the Military and Naval officers the case is somewhat different, for though they may get into office through political influence, they are usually appointed for life and are not removed without cause.

After the above come the Clerks or employees of the government, which number several thousand in Washington alone. They are, in reality, the hardest working population of the Metropolis. Among them may be found men from every State in the Union, and from many foreign countries. [They are] men of no particular mark who have lost fortunes; ripe scholars who have been rudely buffeted by the work; men of capacity who can teach their superiors in office; rare penmen and common-place accountants; and a sisterhood, composed chiefly of respectable widows and orphans who have fled to the Government for support. The custom of employing women as clerks originated out of the disasters which followed the late [Civil War], and the number now employed by the Government has already reached several thousand, and they have been found to be quite as useful as men-clerks. Their compensation ranges from nine hundred to twenty-five hundred dollars per annum, and while it is true that many receive more than they earn because of their idle or inattentive habits, others find it difficult to secure a comfortable support. Occasionally a man may be found who has grown gray in the public service, and is an oracle. But the great majority are, in reality, a floating population. The comparative ease with which these clerks earn their money tends to make them improvident. Many instances might be mentioned, however, where clerks have left the government service and become as distinguished as merchants, or in some of the professions.

For a totally different phase of Washington life, and the most influential for evil or for good, we must turn to the brotherhood of Congressmen. Coming as they do from all parts of the country, and representing every variety of population, it is quite as impossible to speak of them collectively as of their individual characteristics. Among them are to be found honest and able statesmen; but that a large proportion of them are mere time-serving politicians is a fact that cannot be questioned. It is frequently the case that after a Congressman has ended his career as a legislator, he turns office-seeker and many of them, without a knowledge of any language but their own, are sent abroad as diplomatic Ministers. Of these Congressmen, there have been not less than five thousand of them elected since the foundation of the Government. . . . [T]he several political parties to which they have belonged may be summed up as Federalists, Democrats, Whigs, Locofocos, Freesoilers, Abolitionists, Fire-eaters, Republicans, Copperheads, Native Americans, Secessionists, and Radicals, forming in the aggregate a conglomeration of political ideas quite in keeping with the energetic and free spirit of the American people. Prior to the late Civil War, colored men were not admitted to seats in Congress, but at the present time a few of them hold positions in both Houses of Congress—there being now no distinction recognized on account of color, so far as political rights are concerned.

With regard to the permanent population of Washington, little can be said of special interest. Occupying, as this city does, a position on the River Potomac, at the head of navigation, about midway between the Atlantic Ocean and the Allegheny Mountains, it was calculated to become a place of commercial importance. But this idea was not realized, and it became a metropolitan city, chiefly dependent for its support upon the General Government. The local trade is measured by the wants of the population, and there is nothing exported excepting a limited amount of flour, and a considerable quantity of bituminous coal. The only particular . . . in which the inhabitants differ from those of other American cities is in their free and easy manners, growing out of their intercourse and familiarity with people from all quarters of the globe, drawn hither by business or pleasure. With them, the dignitaries of the land, as well as ambassadors from abroad, are appreciated at their real value. And a man who towers as a giant in the rural districts, is very sure to be measured accurately in the metropolis.

But the most peculiar feature of Washington society at the present time (1871), is the position to which the colored or negro population has attained. Before the late Civil War, these unhappy people were in a state of bondage, and only enough of them were congregated in the metropolis to supply the demand for household servants. While the war was progressing, which resulted in their emancipation, large numbers fled to this city as to a place of refuge, and here a large proportion of them have continued to remain to the present time. They have been admitted to all the rights and privileges of citizenship. But while the more intelligent have profited by their advantages, large numbers of them are content to idle away their time, or depend upon the authorities for support, and they constitute about one-third of the present population. They have not as yet been sufficiently educated to be received in society on the same footing with the white race, and the repugnance to receiving them at the same table or to intermarrying with them, is as strong as in other times quite universal, and will probably so continue.

In the further prosecution of our plan, we must direct attention to that large mass of the community engaged in carrying on the business of the nation in the diverse regions of the United States. We begin with the Postmasters, one of whom is located in every city, town, and village throughout the land, and the aggregate number of whom is about twenty-six thousand, exclusive of their numerous assistants. Their duties are, to receive and deliver all letters sent to their several offices, and to look after the prompt dispatch of the mails, by ships and railroads, by coaches and wagons, and on horseback. Their compensation ranges from six thousand dollars to a few dollars per annum. They are all appointed indirectly by the President and hold office during his pleasure. Next to these come the custom-house officers who, including all grades, number not less than five thousand employees. After these comes another large body whose business is to collect the Internal Revenue of the country; and also a very extensive force engaged in carrying on the interests connected with the Public Lands, the Indian Tribes, and the Judicial business in the various States and Territories, as well as those interests prosecuted under the authority of the Patent Office, the Pension Office, and the Agricultural Department.

Now, as the people [above] mentioned, numbering in the gross not far from sixty thousand persons, obtain their positions through political influence, it is natural that they should take a special interest in politics, and do their utmost for the success of the particular party to which they belong. Hence the great excitement which invariably prevails at all the elections. As before intimated, the President and Vice-President are voted for once in every four years; and the Representatives in Congress once in every four years; and the Representatives in Congress once in two years. The Senators being chosen by the State Legislatures. It would appear, therefore, that as the people are intelligent and honest, so must be the office-holders. But this is not always the case because of the existence of what are called mere politicians or demagogues. This class of citizens has greatly multiplied of late years, and it is safe to say that nearly all the troubles which befall the country are the result of their petty schemes and selfish intrigues. There is not a village in the land where they do not congregate, or pursue in secret their unpatriotic designs. Of course there are many exceptions to this state of things. But the rule is as we have stated it, and the evils resulting from the power thus obtained and prostituted, have come to be universally recognized and deplored by the honest people of the land. The loss of dignity is today a source of mortification and alarm among the virtuous and patriotic citizens of the country. The philosophy of government is a subject to which the people of America have devoted but little attention, and yet it is claimed that they are in advance of all other nations in the practice of self-government. To what extent this is true, the present writer is not called upon to decide. It is too true, however, that the opinion is frequently expressed by foreigners that the unbridled system of a Republican government leads to many political troubles.

The two or three crowning features of the American Government would seem to be as follows: That the nation is a peculiar organism, having a life and destiny of its own, founded on the idea of humanity, and like the individual person, but in a more continuous degree. [The] authority to govern the people is derived from their actual or implied assent; and that, in asserting its prerogatives, it looks to the least possible interference with the free action of the individuals composing the community. This form of government involves the idea of contract, tacit or expressed, and no matter how it may be carried out must rest upon the understanding of the people, not only as to the end to be pursued, but also as to the methods. As one circle within another, so does the government of each State and Territory revolve within the circle of the Union, and the State, county, and town elections, for offices which are subject to State patronage, are precisely similar in character and results to the National elections.

While deprecating the abuses to which the American people are subject, on account of what is called universal suffrage, there are many social features which are to be highly commended, and are peculiar to the country. Among these [are] the absence of pauperism, and the universal respectability in per-

propriate employments, from a government clerkship to a claim agency. The only one of the Presidents who consented to enter Congress after leaving the Executive Chair was John Quincy Adams; but his character stood so high as a man and a statesman [that] he could afford to do as he pleased and to die, as he did, in the harness of public life.

As before stated, the total number of men who have served the country as law-makers is about five thousand. Of these the legal profession has sent the largest proportion; the men of letters have numbered only one in every fifty; the eloquent speakers, or orators of special note, have not been more than two hundred. Less than one-half graduated at learned institutions; while the balance have been farmers and planters, merchants, and members of various professions. The total number of men who have held Cabinet appointments is one hundred and eighty-two, of whom one hundred and thirty-three have been Congressmen. Of the forty-four Supreme Court Judges, one-half of them served in the Senate or House of Representatives. Out of five hundred and twenty-seven foreign Ministers, one hundred and seventy were members of Congress. And of the seven hundred and sixty-eight State and Territorial Governors, three hundred and forty-nine were Congressmen.

The treaty which has recently been made between the American and English Governments consummates a long-wished-for condition of affairs: a cordial good-will with all the great Powers of Europe—Great Britain, France, Germany, Italy, Russia, and Spain. It is claimed, indeed, by the best thinkers that the American Government was never more powerful and influential for good than it is at the present time. Intercourse and trade between the two continents, over the Pacific Ocean, are growing rapidly. The friendship of Japan for the United States, and its thorough reciprocation on their part, are universally acknowledged. The latter seem to watch attentively the movements of England and other European Powers in the Far East. And while the British Government may deem it wise to use force in its dealings with the eastern nations, the American policy appears to adhere resolutely to the principles of peace, justice, and equal rights to all, notwithstanding the late unwarranted operations of the American Navy on the coast of Korea [in 1866 and 1871].

The changes for good that have taken place in Japan during the last few years are a matter of wonder and satisfaction to the whole civilized world. The American people have been, since the memorable visit of Commodore Perry, taking great and special interest in the affairs of Japan. The President of the United States has justly echoed the prevailing sentiment among the Americans when he said to the Prince Fushimi, member of one of the Imperial families of the Mikado [Emperor], that he had seen with pride the young men of Japan coming over to receive their education, and that he would take the greatest pleasure in contriving to make their residence in this country both agreeable and useful to them. There rests upon Japan a great hope, as well as high responsibility, for the success of bringing about a healthy and exemplary civilization, which must take the lead among all Asiatic nations.

P.S. In view of the changes which are constantly taking place among the officials of the American Government to which allusion has been made in the foregoing pages, the writer must express an opinion. They are, beyond all question, a great disadvantage to the Republic. They naturally interfere with the proper and regular working of the machinery of the Government, and are the primary cause of the bitter political dissensions which have long prevailed, and continue to prevail, among the American people. And what is more, they lead to all kinds of corruption; and at the very time of our writing these lines, the people of New York are greatly convulsed over the discovery that the Treasury of the City and State has been robbed to the extent of many millions of dollars, growing directly out of the evils of office-seeking, and rotation in office, from party considerations. On the other hand, it must be confessed that where the people have it in their power, as in America, to regulate the conduct of the men they elect to office, so long as they are truly honest, they can always prevent a long continuance of the evils brought upon them by unscrupulous demagogues. Hence the great importance of their being both virtuous and truly patriotic.

Chapter Two

Life among the Farmers and Planters

In the present paper we propose to give a comprehensive account of the agricultural population of the United States, and shall speak of farm life in New England (the Eastern), the Middle, and Western States, and of plantation life in the Southern States. It is now generally acknowledged that the prosperity of America depends chiefly upon its agriculture, and that it has come to be considered the granary of Europe.

The area of land susceptible of cultivation has been estimated to be about 2,250,000,000 [two billion, two hundred and fifty million] acres, more than half of which is owned by the Government. Five hundred million acres [of these] having been surveyed and are now ready for occupation, while the lands under cultivation amount to more than two hundred million acres. It has also been estimated that seven-eighths of the entire population of the country are engaged in agricultural pursuits, or in the various professions and trades naturally dependent thereupon. The largest wheat crop ever produced in the States was in 1869, when the yield amounted to two hundred and sixty-four millions (264,000,000) of bushels, and, as the average price was one dollar and forty cents ($1.40), the total cash value was not less than $369,600,000. The quantity of corn was 1,100,000,000 bushels; rye, 22,000,000; barley, 28,000,000; buckwheat, 17,000,000; oats, 275,000,000, and potatoes, 111,000,000; hay, 22,000,000 tons; tobacco, 310,000,000 pounds; cane sugar, 120,000,000 pounds, and cotton, 1,767,000,000 pounds, valued at $147,380,000. And as to domestic animals, including young cattle, horses, sheep, and swine, their value was $978,872,785.

With these few leading facts before him, the reader may obtain an approximate idea of the agricultural wealth of the country, and he must remember that the very numerous unmentioned articles would swell the agricultural supplies to the extent of many additional millions. It is claimed by English farmers that, in some particulars, their method of farming is superior to that practiced in this country and that is undoubtedly true. But, on the other hand, it has been demonstrated that the leading grains can be produced at a much lower cost in the United States than in England. As this is pre-eminently an agricultural country, it follows that here the most numerous attempts to produce labor-saving implements have been directed to facilitate the labors of the farm. The extent to which new agricultural inventions have been patented is so great that in 1869 they reached the number of nineteen hundred (1,900), and all of them for saving muscular power on the farm and in the household. . . . In the more settled parts of the country the old-fashioned varieties of the hoe, the spade, and even the ploughshare, are now looked upon as barbarous contrivances, and in their place the farmers use what are called steam-ploughs, the rotary spade, the sulky-plough, horse-cultivators, shovel-ploughs, as well as reaping, mowing, and threshing machines, of many varieties. The improvements that have been made in such tools as the shovel, spade, hoe, and fork, are so great that they may almost be considered entirely new inventions. With regard to these and many other implements of husbandry in America, lightness, simplicity, and comparative cheapness are absolutely essential to their perfection. One of the effects, if not the most important, of these labor-saving machines has been that while one man has been kept in the field, three have been sent to the great towns to prosecute other enterprises of profit, or have entered upon the cultivation of other farms. The organization of Agricultural Societies, which have done much to perfect the science of tilling the soil, was commenced shortly after the establishment of the Government in 1776. Their influence, in connection with annual fairs, has been widespread and of the greatest advantage. There is not a State in the Union which does not boast of one of them, organized for the benefit of all the inhabitants at large. Nor ought the fact to be forgotten, that there are already many Agricultural Colleges in the country, and that they are annually increasing in numbers and influence. And then, again, the agricultural periodicals are numerous and of high repute.

But notwithstanding all these facts, experienced men have expressed the opinion that the condition of agriculture in this country is not what might be desired. The great trouble is the want of proper method. The art is as yet imperfectly known and practiced, and the American system is full of deficiencies. The domain of the United States embraces soil capable of yielding the riches and most varied productions, in the greatest abundance. It is a peculiar feature of the country that all the lands which have been sold by the Government, or are still owned by the same, are surveyed upon a system of squares and divided into townships of six miles square, subdivided into sections and quarter sections whereby the farms are generally regular in shape, and disputes are avoided in regard to boundary lines. The lands belonging to the

Government are sold at the uniform price of one dollar and a quarter ($1.25) per acre, so that for one hundred dollars a new settler can receive a farm of eighty acres. But under existing laws, a foreigner, as well as a native, if of age and intending to become a citizen, obtains a homestead substantially as a free gift.[1] The total quantity of land owned by the Government was 1,834,968,400 acres; of which 447,266,190 acres have been sold; and the amount now for sale is 1,387,732,209 acres. That the National Government takes a deep interest in the welfare of the agricultural population is proven by the fact that a Department of Agriculture exists in Washington, which annually publishes a very valuable volume of miscellaneous information, and supplies seeds and cuttings for all who may apply for them, while the postal laws of the country allow their transportation through the mails free of expense; the same laws making only a small charge for the exchange of seeds, cuttings, and plants between private parties. But more than all that, the National Government has recently made a grant of seven millions (7,000,000) of acres of land for the benefit of Agricultural Colleges, and propositions are now pending for giving away nearly twenty millions (20,000,000) acres of land for objects directly or indirectly connected with the farming population of the Republic.[2] The total number of farms in the United States is about three millions, which gives a farm for every thirteen of the entire population, and the largest proportion of these farms range from twenty to one hundred acres.

FARM LIFE IN NEW ENGLAND

And now we propose to give a description in general terms of farm life in the New England States (the six Eastern States): Maine, Massachusetts, New Hampshire, Vermont, Connecticut, and Rhode Island. In this region the farms are almost universally small, ranging from ten to one hundred acres, and stone-fences predominate above all other kinds. The agricultural season is short, winter lasting through half the year. No verdure but that of evergreens resists the annual cold, and an unmelted mass of snow covers the ground for months. The soils, excepting in the more extensive valleys, are poor and rocky, and aside from those farms which are given up chiefly to the grazing of cattle or the production of hay, the products of the earth are only obtained by the severest kind of labor. Along the seashore, kelp and fish are popular

---

1. Some foreigners in Western states and territories, especially Chinese, were usually denied the right to own farmland by state and local laws.

2. The Morrill Land Grant Act of 1862 donated public lands to states and territories for the purpose of establishing agricultural colleges.

manures; but in the interior, guano, calcareous manures, and the yield of the barn-yards are employed. The owner is, himself, the foremost workman, and his sons [are] his principal assistants. And all household matters are performed by the females of the family. The farmers live in comfortable frame houses, very frequently surrounded with flowers, use both coal and wood for fuel, and are noted for their frugality and neatness. Their barns are spacious and substantial. They produce nothing for exportation, but a greater variety of crops than the more extensive farmers, and are quite content if they can obtain a plain, comfortable support. In Vermont, the raising of superior breeds of horses has been a specialty, but for farmwork, oxen are more popular than horses. If the farmers happen to have a small surplus of any commodity, they dispose of it [sell] in a neighboring town; and thus provide themselves with luxuries, or put aside a little money for a rainy day. In some localities agriculture is often joined to other employments, such as fishing and shoemaking.

The farmers in New England, as well as throughout the country, are generally a reading people, and profit somewhat by the published theories on the science of agriculture. Their children have access to the country schools, but the sons are often obliged to help their parents in the field during the vernal months, so that their principal time for study is in the winter. They are a church-going people, and, to the extent of their means, liberal in furthering the cause to which they may be attached. They take an interest in politics, and are decided in their opinions. They are social in their dispositions, fond of visiting their friends, and on winter evenings have what they call apple-paring and bed-quilting frolics, when their homes are cheered by such refreshments as mince and pumpkin pies, as well as cider, walnuts, and apples. Their amusements are as various as their tastes, but the perpetual struggle with mother earth for the means of living makes them careful of their time and is apt to induce and keep alive the most serious views of life. On farms lying in the vicinity of villages it is often the case that certain members of the family obtain positions in the factories or other manufacturing establishments, whereby they are enabled to increase their means of support. As soon as the boys attain the age of manhood, they find their fields of operation circumscribed, and leaving the paternal roof, wander forth into the world to make their own fortunes. Some of them [travel] to the turmoil and strife of the large cities, and others to the more inviting regions of the great, and not yet fully developed [American] West. In New England farm life is today very much what it was a generation ago, and from the very nature of the cold and barren soil, will so continue without any marked progress. The farmers have done their best, in fact all that could be done. Everything is finished, and they are content. It is not that the spirit of competition has died out there. That the agricultural interests of New England have reached and passed the period of culmination is undoubtedly true. The farmers of this region are more truly the yeomanry of the land than any other class, and a large proportion of them are natives of the soil they now cultivate. And, like the venerable oaks and elms which adorn many of their farms, they are content to live in the present as in the past, hoping that any family offshoots that may have been planted in more congenial and productive soils will be, as they have been in unnumbered instances, a blessing to their descendants.

FARM LIFE IN THE MID-ATLANTIC STATES

We now pass over into what are called the four Middle States of the Union: New York, Pennsylvania, New Jersey, and Delaware, where we shall find a somewhat different condition of affairs, but with the stamp of New England manners and customs everywhere visible. There the average size of farms is between one hundred and one hundred and fifty acres, and, generally speaking, the soil is productive. The fences are usually made of rails, and every variety of manure is employed. If not rich, the farmers are in easy circumstances, and count upon annually laying up something handsome in the way of profits. Though well posted in their business by years of practical experience, they employ a needed supply of hands who do most of the hard work while their own time is occupied with the lighter duties of the farm and a general supervision of affairs. Their houses are comfortable and often elegant, and afford ample accommodation for the proprietor, his family, and his assistants. While those of New York, where the native American element prevails, fare sumptuously on the food of their own raising, and have become celebrated for their superior butter and cheese, the farmers of Dutch descent, located in Pennsylvania, are charged with never eating what might be readily sold at the nearest market. It is to the credit of these farmers that their barns are unequaled in this country, oftentimes better than the houses they live in, and that with them, the profits of their style of farming are always satisfactory. With regard to the cheese business, it has come to be so extensive that we may allude to it more particularly. The entire produce of last year was about one hundred millions of pounds, three-fourths of which was made in the Middle States, but the largest amount in New York.

From time immemorial the Dutch have had control of this business, but the exports from this country are now about double of the exports from Holland. Formerly it was the custom of the farmers to make cheese upon their respective farms, but it is now made in regularly established factories, which are supported by the farmers located in their vicinity. The total number of these factories now flourishing in this country is thirteen hundred, and they are supplied with milk from not less than three hundred thousand cows. In New Jersey and Delaware, and on Long Island, where the chief attention is devoted to fruits and vegetables, and where are to be found the most beautiful gardens in the country, the hired hands are more numerous than elsewhere, in proportion to the size of the farms or gardens, but their positions are not so permanent. Various kinds of berries are here raised in the greatest abundance, and the surplus hands left unemployed after the annual gatherings have to seek other employment.

In the great majority of cases, the proprietor joins his hired men in the work to be done, whether in casting the seed, driving the machinery employed, or gathering in the harvests. They all occupy the same platform as citizens, whether naturalized, or natives of the country: free access to schools and churches is enjoyed by all, without regard to family or fortune. The man who is working today as a hired hand knows full well that if he continues to be true to himself and his opportunities, he will yet be respected as a proprietor. By means of newspapers and books, they keep up with the spirit of the age, and, though generally disinclined to participate in the partisan squabbles of the day, they are by no means indifferent to the welfare of the country, and are frequently called upon to fill offices of trust and honor. They rise early, eat a frugal meal at noon, and retire at the coming on of darkness, excepting in the winter, which is their time for visiting and home enjoyment; and this is true of the farming classes generally throughout the country. What are called fancy farmers are probably more numerous in the Middle States than in any other region, but these men are apt to spend more money than they make. An idea of the wealth which some of them attain may be gathered from the fact that there is one family in the Valley of the Genesee in New York, who own not less than thirty thousand acres of land, and all of it in the highest state of cultivation. It is this class of the more wealthy farmers, residing in all the States, who greatly benefit the country by introducing the best kinds of stock from foreign countries, who have been known to pay twenty thousand dollars for a single stallion (horse), two or three thousand for a heifer, a ram, or a bull, or one hundred dollars for a trio of fowls, consisting of one male and two females. It was one of these extensive farmers who inaugurated the plan of issuing printed cards with the following regulations for the guidance of his men: "Regularity in hours. Punctuality in cleaning and putting away implements. Humanity to all the animals. Neatness and cleanliness in personal appearance. Decency in deportment and conversation. Obedience to the proprietor, and ambition to excel in farming." Extensive and various as are the farming interests of the Middle States, and so great are the temptations to go farther west, the demand for farmhands and female servants is always greater than the supply, and while the men receive from fifteen to thirty dollars per month, with board, the women receive from eight to fifteen dollars per month for housework, and of these, by far the largest proportion are from England, Ireland, and Germany.

The secret of the unparalleled growth and the daily increasing power of the United States is that the Government, in its practical working, is confined to the narrowest limits. It is the agent, not the master of the people, and the latter initiate all changes in its political and social life. It is, therefore, the condition of the success of a settlement that the immigrant relies on his own strength, nets on his own responsibility, and seeks by his own efforts the prosperity which he is sure to find if undisturbed. In spite of obstacles and disappointment, he will make his way and ultimately attain his objects.

In the States now under consideration, as well as in all the States of the Union, excepting New York and a few others, a married woman may not convey her separate real estate, except in a joint deed with her husband; and yet, in most of the States, the separate property of the wife is recognized. There is no imprisonment for debt in any part of the Republic. When a farmer has become insolvent (in more than half the States), his homestead is exempt from execution [forfeiture]; and in all of them, household furniture to the extent of five hundred dollars, wearing apparel, tools, and books necessary to carry on business, one to five cows, one yoke of oxen, ten sheep, carts, and farming implements, and the uniform and arms of any man who is or has been in the public service, are also exempt from the grasp of the creditor. When the head of a family dies without making a will, his property is equally divided among his children or their offspring, except that the wife has a life-interest of one-third, called the widow's dower. When there are no lineal descendants the estate goes to the next of kin.

FARM LIFE IN THE WESTERN STATES

The next division of farm life we have to consider is that of the Western States. Of these there are sixteen in all, thirteen in the valley of the Mississippi River, and three on the Pacific Ocean. Their extent is so immense, and their products so numerous, that it is difficult for the mind to comprehend their importance and influence. Four of them were, until recently classed among the Slave States; and because the system of slave labor therein has become greatly modified by free labor, they can hardly be, with propriety, embraced in our present review. As a wheat-producing region, the Western States have progressed in a manner perfectly amazing, until they now stand unsurpassed by any other region of like extent in the world. Although the population has increased about fifty per cent in the last twenty years, the increase of produce has greatly exceeded that of population. But the relative value of all the other cereals and other farm productions in these States is quite as extensive and remarkable as that of wheat. That the people who are annually bringing out of the soil such immense wealth are wide-awake and industrious is self-evident. Generally speaking, the farms are much larger than those in the

Middle States, and the farmhands very much more numerous. Very many of the farmers with whom we come in contact seem to have settled in the country with limited means. Some bought land with no more money than would pay the first installment on it, and had to work for others to make money to pay the other installments as they came due. They are able, in this way, in a few years to settle down and cultivate their own soil, and this method of operating is in progress today. When farms are rented, which is often done, the system adopted is as follows: If the tenant is not able to provide stock, implements, and seeds, the proprietor supplies him with all these, and then allows him one-third of the grain-crops. In this way many a man works himself into a farm of his own. The ordinary rate of interest on borrowed money is ten per cent, but even at this high rate it usually pays a farmer well, and there is every facility given to respectable and industrious men. There are often cultivated farms in the market for sale, but persons desiring to purchase cannot always be present; and, in buying second-hand farms, it is well to be certain that it has not been previous mortgaged.

As is the case in all other branches of business, the man who has the best capacity is likely to be the most successful, and the operations of some of the more famous farmers in the West sound more like romance than reality. For example, there was lately one farm in Illinois which contained about forty thousand acres, with one pasture-field of eight thousand acres. Its chief production was corn, all of which was consumed upon the farm itself. In one year the proprietor sent to New York City cattle enough to bring seventy thousand dollars, while his home stock was valued at one million dollars. Yet, the man lived in a small house, in the most simple and unpretending style, and habitually sat down at the same table with his hired men. But the farming exploits of this man were eclipsed subsequently by those of another, who is now carrying on a farm of fifty thousand acres. With regard to another of the model farms of Illinois, we may state that it contains thirty-six thousand acres, and last year had one cornfield of five thousand five hundred acres, yielding two hundred and twenty thousand bushels, three thousand tons of hay, four thousand head of cattle, and gave employment to eighty-five ploughs, fifteen planting machines, and fifteen mowing machines. The hedge fencing on this farm measures about one hundred and thirty miles, and contains also about eight miles of board fencing. There is, however, still another farm, located in Illinois, which ought to be mentioned in this place, as it is reputed to be one of the most extensive and successful in the world. It is called the Burr Oak Farm, and is owned by a man named Sullivan. It embraces sixty-five square miles, and although the owner commenced work upon it only four years ago, he has at the present time growing upon it not less than eleven thousand acres of corn, and five thousand acres . . . in miscellaneous crops. The hedges which cross, re-cross, and surround the farm, measure three hundred miles, the board fences six miles, and the ditches one hundred and fifty miles. The workingmen employed on this farm are mostly Swedes and Germans, number two hundred and fifty, and are constantly employed from the first of April to the first of January. They work ten hours per day, report to the proprietor every evening, and are not allowed the use of intoxicating drinks. The working animals of the farm consist of three hundred and fifty yoke of oxen, and it is amply supplied with the ordinary stock of an extensive farm. The leading machinery employed consists of one hundred and fifty steel ploughs, seventy-five breaking ploughs; one hundred and forty-two cultivators; forty-five corn-planters, and twenty-five harrows; and it has one ditching plough which is drawn by sixty-eight oxen and managed by eight men. The house in which the proprietor resides is a common wooden structure, comfortable, but without the least pretension. It will be understood, of course, that farms of this extent are not found in every county or State, but they give us an idea of the spirit that animates the farming fraternity generally.

Let us now look at the operations of one or two small farmers in Illinois. One man, for example, purchased eighty acres of prairie land for $360; spent $500 on improvements; his crops for the first year brought him over $1,500, and at the close of the third year his farm was sold for $2,000. Another man, with a capital of only $700, bought one hundred and sixty acres. His annual produce for six years was $2,000, at the end of which time he was worth about ten thousand dollars. And such instances as the above have occurred by the thousands in the great West.

As we glance over the immense number of farmers who are toiling throughout the Western States, it is quite impossible to depict their manners and customs with anything like accuracy. So many are the nationalities which compose the great mass of inhabitants, the mere mention of these is indeed a kind of description. In Illinois and Ohio, the Germans, Irish, and English are about equally divided; in Wisconsin the English and Germans predominate; and Missouri is most extensively settled by the Germans. In the States bordering on the Great Lakes and the Upper Mississippi several Scandinavian colonies have been established; and there has been a considerable immigration of Chinese into California, but this latter class has not manifested any strong predisposition for agricultural pursuits.[3] The great variety of nationalities which sometimes

---

3. At this time, many Chinese in California were working in mines and many had just finished working on the transcontinental railroad, which was completed in 1869. The number of Chinese agricultural laborers was dramatically increasing, and they would significantly contribute to the development of California agriculture for the rest of the nineteenth century. See Sucheng Chan, *This Bittersweet Soil: The Chinese in California Agriculture, 1860–1910* (Berkeley: University of California Press, 1986).

congregate in one region, was strikingly exemplified a few years ago when the State of Wisconsin was obliged to publish its Governor's message in not less than eight languages. The amount of money sent across the ocean by immigrants, to friends left behind, principally to pay their passage to America, is surprising. From the official returns of Emigration Commissioners of England, it appears that in 1870 there were sent from this country to Ireland . . . $3,630,040 in gold, of which $1,663,190, was for pre-paid passage. In the twenty-three years from 1848 to 1870, the amount of money sent was $81,670,000 in gold, being an average of about $3,889,047 yearly. But this amount is probably somewhat below the actual amount as it only includes what has been sent through banks and commercial houses. And these sums, large as they are, are made up by careful savings from the wages of servant girls and farm laborers.

In California, Missouri, and Ohio, the grape has been so extensively cultivated as to give them the reputation of being the wine-producing regions of the United States. Among their vineyards we find many of the habits prevailing which are common to the wine districts of Europe. In California a farm is called a ranch, and one of the most noted ones in that State may be described as follows. [This ranch] contains eighteen thousand (18,000) acres; and last year sixteen hundred (1,600) acres were devoted to wheat, eight hundred (800) to barley, two hundred (200) to oats, two hundred (200) to meadow, and about fifteen thousand (15,000) acres to orchards, vineyards, and pasturage. The fruit trees number eight thousand (8,000) the grapevines fifty-thousand (50,000); and the livestock consists of two hundred (200) horses, one thousand (1,000) head of cattle, three thousand (3,000) sheep, and two thousand (2,000) swine; and the entire domain is surrounded with good fences.

From the above and other facts already narrated, it will be seen that the United States are supplied with all kinds of farmers; some cultivating their thousands of acres, and others their half dozen. Yet they all seem to live comfortably, and the great majority are independent. And there are numerous instances of American women who have been, and are today, quite successful in the management of farms. [However], what will be the result upon the agricultural and industrial interests of the extensive emigration from China to this country now going on is a problem which can only be settled by the future.[4]

---

4. According to United States government census records, there were 58,325 Chinese in the United States in 1870, and 100,038 by 1880. In 1882, the U.S. Congress prohibited the immigration of Chinese laborers with the Chinese Exclusion Act, which was renewed in 1892 and extended indefinitely in 1902. Despite exceptions for students, teachers, businessmen, and family members, Chinese were effectively prohibited from emigrating to the United States from 1882 until after World War II.

FARM LIFE IN THE SOUTHERN STATES

Our next subject for consideration is the plantation life of the Southern States. Only about six years have now passed away since the close of the Civil War, which resulted in the emancipation of more than four millions of slaves. A glance at the condition of the South, before the great event, would seem to be necessary. In 1860 there were fifteen States in which slavery existed, and all of them, excepting five, made war upon the General Government—four of them having already been mentioned as among the Western States. They contained a population of 4,334,250, of whom only 383,637 were slave owners. The number of plantations under cultivation was estimated at 765,000, comprehending about 75,000,000 of acres. . . . The planter was the owner, not only of broad acres almost without number, but also of from ten to one thousand menials or slaves, whom he fed and clothed for his own exclusive profit . . . and who, for the most part, did his bidding without a murmur or thought beyond the passing hour. He lived at his case, among books and in the dispensation of a liberal hospitality, leaving all the labor on his plantation to the direction of an overseer who spent most of his time on horseback, issuing orders to the working men and women, and watching the regular progress of affairs. According to his wealth, the planter lived in a house or an elegant mansion, while his slaves were domiciled in rude but comfortable cabins. They received a supply of provisions, but no compensation in money, although it was customary to allow them the use of a patch of ground for their own benefit and a fragment of time out of each day or week to cultivate it.

But all this is now changed. Slave labor has no existence on the soil of the United States, and the opinion is universal that the suppression of slave labor will ultimately add greatly to the national advancement of all the States in which it formerly existed. Among the results following the late rebellion was the fact that much of the property in the Southern States passed into new hands. Many old plantations were abandoned by their owners and have never been reclaimed, others have been confiscated, and others sold at a ruinous sacrifice. Many of the soldiers who went South, who had been raised among the rocky hills of the North, became in love with the rich and beautiful fields and valleys of the South and thousands resolved to settle in the new country. They married Southern women, formed new alliances and associations, and have opened up a new career for the South, which is rapidly becoming more and more salutary in its influences. The great landed estates which have been cut up, may be purchased by all newcomers at a very small cost. [Meanwhile] the black race, to a great extent, have settled upon small patches of land where they can maintain themselves in comfort, and enjoy an independence of thought and feeling which they did not know under the old order of things. Whole plantations have been settled by families of owners, who were formerly

slaves upon the same estates. Men who were formerly overseers or superin-
tendents, are themselves settling down upon their own newly-acquired farms.
Although attempts to obtain laborers from China and Sweden have been made,
the principal cultivators of the Southern States are the Freedmen, who, indo-
lent by nature, do as little work as possible, will not hire out for more than a
single year, and one of the results of their freedom is that they will not let their
wives work as in the olden times. To retain their services, the planter is obliged
to praise and humor them in many ways. The terms upon which the Negroes
are hired is generally to let them have one-half of what they produce, but when
supported by the planter they receive but one-quarter of what they produce.
When the planters are attentive to their business they almost invariably succeed, and when unsuccessful as farmers, they are apt to help their pockets by
keeping small country stores.

In all the towns are located men who are called warehouse men, whose
business is to receive, store, and sell all the cotton or other produce which
may be consigned to their care. What the people of the South now need is
help—not lands; and in many of the most fertile regions, every inducement is
thrown out to invite emigration from the North. But it is idle to suppose that
the griefs, the passions, and animosities engendered by the late rebellion, will
die out while the present generation survives. Too many brave men have per-
ished, too many homes made desolate, too many families broken up and reduced to beggary, to expect anything of that sort. Men whom it has impover-
ished will live and die poor, remembering constantly the cause of their
poverty. Widows will long mourn over husbands, children over fathers, slain
in battle. A new and happier era is in store for the rising generation, but its advance will be slow. The people of the North and of the South, it is fondly
hoped and believed, will again become a happy, a united, and prosperous people; united in interests, in pursuits, in intelligence, and in patriotic devotion to
their united country.

Of all the products grown in the Southern States the most important and
universal is cotton, and it has been asserted that it was this single commodity
which prevented that portion of the Union from relapsing into abject poverty.
Everything was sacrificed to slavery, and slavery sacrificed everything to itself. As there were not slaves enough to cultivate the soil as it needed, cotton-
raising was all that saved the country. The principal States where cotton is
now grown are Mississippi, Alabama, Louisiana, Georgia, Texas, and
Arkansas, and in all of them efforts are being made for the introduction of
Chinese labor. The cultivation of rice is limited to three States, South Carolina, Georgia, and Louisiana; sugarcane and its products—in the way of
sugar and molasses—to Louisiana. In Florida considerable attention is paid to
the cultivation of oranges, lemons, and other tropical fruits. Wheat and to-

bacco have occupied the chief attention of farmers in Virginia and the neighboring States of Tennessee and Kentucky. North Carolina has acquired a reputation for its sweet potatoes and groundnuts. Indian corn is an important product in all the Southern States while the mountain-lands, which in all directions are covered with grass as well as extensive forests, are devoted to the grazing of cattle in great numbers, where they flourish throughout the year without shelter or any special care. In all the States lying directly on the Gulf of Mexico the climate is mild, the winters short, open, and delightful, and farmwork can be done every month in the year. They begin there to make their gardens in December, and until the following December there is a continuous succession of crops. The people live easily, and produce more for the same amount of labor than in any of the Northern States. Lands are cheap, and may often be paid for by a single crop. The timber is everywhere magnificent, and the lands are irrigated by numerous streams, and adapted to an unlimited variety of products.

For the raising of cattle there is not a region, probably, in the world, better suited for that purpose than the extensive State of Texas. In some localities, the cattle may be counted by the thousand, and it is an amazing fact that droves of them are annually sent by the stock-raisers as far off as California. Texas cattle have even been butchered in the city of New York, and even cargoes of Texas beef have been shipped in ice to Philadelphia. From ten to twelve men are required for a herd of a thousand cattle, with two horses or mules to each man, for day and night duty; the cattle needing to be herded at night to prevent stampedes. For those who have never witnessed its operations, it is difficult to realize the extent of this cattle traffic, and it is sometimes the case that the whole earth seems to be covered with the herds, as far as the eye can reach over the vast prairies. The class of people commonly known as the "Texas Cowboys" are indeed a power in the land, whose exploits and lives of adventure are more like romance than reality. . . .

AMUSEMENTS AND FESTIVALS

Having now taken a general survey of the agricultural population of America, we shall conclude . . . with a few remarks on their manners and customs, as exemplified by certain amusements which are, for the most, peculiar to this country. And first, as to the *sugar-making frolics*. In various parts of the Union, large quantities of sugar are annually made from the sap of the maple-tree. The moment Winter breaks, and the sap begins to ascend in the spring, the trees are tapped, and the liquid thus obtained is boiled down until it becomes a rich syrup or granulated sugar. All this takes place in the dense woods, and most of the work is performed at night. At the close of the season the farmers invite their friends and neighbors to a kind of jubilee, which is held in the sugar-camps, and where, with sumptuous fare, followed by music and dancing, the entire night is given to enjoyment. When the last cauldron of sugar has been made, and daylight has appeared, the company is dispersed, and the sugar utensils are packed away until the coming of another season.

Corresponding to the above, in most of the corn-growing regions they have what are called *"Corn-Huskings."* This entertainment occurs when a farmer is anxious to prepare for market an unusual quantity of the yellow maize. In the North or West, when the young men and country lasses have met, they are piloted to the spacious and sweet-smelling barn, and for a stated time all work without ceasing, until the allotted task is performed. An adjournment then takes place to the farm-house, where feasting and dancing continue all the night long. When this frolic occurs in the South, the colored people there do the work, and enjoy themselves in their own rude but amusing ways, while the white people for whom they may happen to be working, act as the hosts, content to enjoy the laughable scenes brought to view.

In the New England States, especially those regions bordering on the sea, they have what are called *"Clam-Bakes."* These are usually attended by men only, who congregate from various quarters, for the purpose of exchanging political opinions, and having a systematic good time. Speeches are delivered, and large quantities of cheering beverages are imbibed, as well as clams eaten, after a primitive fashion. The shell-fish are roasted in an open field, and duly prepared with the desired condiments. These affairs take place in the summer, after the leading harvests have been gathered in.

In the Southern States certain festivals are common, but more so before the late war than now, which are known as *"Barbecues."* They are political, and sometimes bring together very large numbers of the planters and their families, and the time is generally devoted to speech-making, happily varied by eating and drinking the good things of the land. The principal food on these occasions consists of beef or mutton, and the oxen or sheep are roasted entire, over a pit duly prepared, and filled with burning coals. The cooks and eaters are generally Negro men and women, and, as they have the privilege of inviting their own friends, the groves where they assemble present a varied and fantastic scene. The young people have it all their own way, and there is no end to the variety of their amusements.

Another rural custom is known as a *"House-Raising."* This occurs after some farmer has prepared his timber for a new house or barn, when he invites his friends and neighbors to come and help him to lift the timbers and cross-pieces into their proper places. This invitation is always cheerfully accepted, and most of the time is devoted to downright hard work. But after the task has been accomplished, the men have a substantial feast, and a good long talk about their farms, their crops, and cattle, and commonly separate with a warm brotherly feeling for each other and for their fellowmen everywhere.

In some of the fruit-growing regions, large quantities of apples are stripped of their skins, cut into quarter pieces, and hung up to dry for winter use, and in that condition become a source of revenue. Out of this variety of business has grown an autumnal festival called an *"Apple-Paring."* This takes place in the evening. The guests are invited as to an ordinary party, and after a few hours' attention to business, the night is given up to feasting and dancing, or the playing of innocent games by the young people, who compose the majority.

Ball-playing and *Sleigh-riding* are two other pastimes in which the Americans indulge with rare gusto. By the rural population Saturday afternoon is usually assigned to the former, on which occasions the young men are as active and expert in throwing and catching, or striking the ball, as if they had been idle all the previous week, instead of having had to work in the fields with the utmost energy. Sleigh-riding, of course, takes place in the winter only, when the ground is covered with snow, and then it is that the young farmers bring out their best horses, fill their sleighs with lady friends, enveloped in gayly trimmed furs, and, to the exhilarating music of the bells, start off on all sorts of expeditions over the neighboring country.

From time immemorial it has been the custom among the Negroes of the South to devote the last week of the year, commonly called *Christmas Holidays*, to every variety of amusement. When slavery existed those prolonged festivities were freely accorded to the slaves, and were full of romantic interest. Now that they are free, the colored people claim their old privilege as a right, but do not find the same unalloyed enjoyment as of old in their annual frolic. They have not as yet arrived at that stage when they can enjoy the blessing of supporting themselves.

About the close of the year they have in various parts of the country what they call *"Shooting Matches."* These are of two kinds; one, where turkeys and other birds are tied to a stake, and made a target for men who like to shoot the rifle, and experienced shots sometimes win a sufficient quantity of large poultry to supply all their friends. Another kind of match is, when two parties pit themselves against each other, and go upon a hunt for a day or a week, for squirrels or birds of game, when the victors are rewarded with a prize of some kind, paid for by the losing party.

And then they have throughout the country such rural jollifications as *Sheep-Shearing, Ploughing Matches*, and, to the discredit of the participants, *Cock-Fightings*, which need not be described.

Of all rural assemblages none are so generally popular as County Fairs. They occur in the Autumn in numerous localities, and bring together thousands of the

agricultural population. The first agricultural Fair ever organized in this country by any of the colored population, was recently carried through with success
in the State of Kentucky. Farm products, animals, and country fabrics are ex-
hibited to a marvelous extent, in many of these Fairs. All sorts of friendly com-
petitions are entered into, and *Horse-racing* has become an important adjunct
to all these Fairs, whether patronized by the State at large or confined to the
counties where they are held.

The crowning custom, and the one most universally recognized by the
American people is the celebration of what is known as *Thanksgiving Day.* It
is an annual festival, honored by proclamations from the President and the local Governors, who specify the particular day.[5] Of all places to enjoy it, none
can be compared to the house of a successful farmer. The primary object of
this festival is to recognize the goodness of the Almighty in crowning the
labors of the field with prosperity, and the occasion is made especially joyous
by the gathering together, under one roof, all the scattered members of the
family in the old home. There are some other rural customs which might be
mentioned in this place, but as they are of a religious character we shall de-
fer them for a subsequent chapter of this volume.

[The following paragraph was originally at the end of *Life and Resources in
America* in a section titled, "Additional Notes."]

In further illustration of the preceding article on agriculture, we append the
following statement: The total value of farm-products in the United States
and Territories, during the year ending June 31, 1870, according to the census, was $2,445,000,000. The largest product was in the State of New York,
and the second largest in Illinois.

---

5. While Thanksgiving had been celebrated since the early seventeenth century by European set-
tlers and their descendants in North America on various days of the year, it was not until 1863 that
Thanksgiving was proclaimed as a national holiday to be held on the fourth Thursday of November.

Chapter Three

Commercial Life and Developments

WATER TRANSPORTATION AND SHIPBUILDING

The inland and coastline navigation of the United States is not surpassed, in extent and character, by any country on the globe. And the industry and enterprise of the Americans, in developing their commercial and shipping interests has been, until within the last few years, equal to their superior advantages. Passing by all statistics in regard to the tonnage of the country, let us take a brief survey of the vessels and navigators which have given the country its reputation.

By far the largest proportion of American vessels are run upon inland waters, and are called small craft; [and] the sea-going vessels, if less numerous, are generally as large as those of any other nation and have been constructed on unsurpassed models. The ships called "Liners," which a few years ago ran between New York and Liverpool, acquired wide celebrity, and have never been surpassed for beauty and speed. But they have been superseded by steamers, and ships of that class now transact the same business. The burthen [displacement] of those sailing-vessels was about two thousand tons. [These vessels] were splendidly equipped, swift, commanded and manned by the best metal [sailors], and did an immense business in bringing merchandise and immigrants to America. But with the calamities that have befallen the mercantile marine of this country, they have nearly all passed away. During the fiscal year of 1870, there were less than one hundred thousand tons of sea-going vessels built in the United States, and less than three hundred thousand tons of all descriptions of vessels, which amount was about equalled by the vessels built on the Clyde alone. Meanwhile, the tonnage of steam-vessels, built all in England, was sixty times greater than that of America. One result of this falling off in American shipbuilding has been that large numbers of men who were brought up on the ocean are seen turning their attention to a variety of pursuits connected wholly with the land. The inland waters of the country are most abundantly supplied with steamboats, and all the varieties of the smaller sailing vessels. The coasting trade and fishing interests are quite as important and extensive as heretofore, but new vessels are by no means now turned out with the rapidity that they were a few years ago. It was the late war [American Civil War] which helped to put back the carrying trade of America, but with the return of peace and the final restoration of the Union, the old order of things began to be restored. When the great rebellion, or rather the British cruisers sailing under its flag, drove American shipping from the seas, and thus transferred the carrying trade to foreign bottoms, the commerce of Philadelphia suffered in common with that of other cities. The substitution of iron for wood at about the same time as the material for first-class steamships, left the country not only without ships, but behind other nations in facilities for making them. Boston, New York, and Baltimore soon recovered in good part their former commerce through the help of foreign subsidized steamship lines. But Philadelphia, more thoroughly imbued with American ideas, made little effort to secure such foreign lines, but waited to build a line of her own, which will soon be established between that city and Liverpool. In 1860 the tonnage of the United States amounted to 5,353,868 tons, and in 1870, to 4,246,507 tons.

COMMERCE AND TRADE

Notwithstanding the above facts, the commerce of the country is very large and flourishing, since it appears that American imports for 1870 amounted to about $600,000,000, and the exports about $400,000,000. The great variety of native productions exported from America gives assurance of the impossibility of failure in the resources of the nation. For example, from the sea they have such products as oil, whalebone, spermaceti, and many kinds, in great abundance of fish. From the forest Americans have timber, shingles, staves, lumber, naval stores, and furs. From agriculture there is every description of corn and vegetable food, and the products of animals in the way of beef, pork, tallow, hides, bacon, cheese, butter, wool, lard, and hams, with horned cattle, horses, and other animals. From the Southern States they have cotton, tobacco, rice, and sugar. From the factories, there is every variety of useful goods. Their exports of specie and bullion have never been exceeded by any other nation. And as to their imports, they are simply enormous—silks, woolen goods, tea, coffee, and sugars being the most important, and for which there has always been a demand.

But the crowning element of American commerce is its internal trade, and in this connection we cannot mention a more remarkable fact than this: the production of spirituous liquors in 1870 amounted to $600,000,000, and the persons engaged in selling it by retail number not less than 150,000. Meanwhile, the importation of opium from China amounted to nearly $2,000,000. The distances in America are so great that the internal trade and traffic of the country has been, and must always be, a business of vast importance. And the extent of territory implies great diversity of productions. The growth of tropical regions are exchanged for the field-crops and forest produce of cooler latitudes; and in another direction, the products of the coast and of extensive interior districts are exchanged. The tide of emigration sets from east to west, while the tide of commerce flows from west to east; and we can only obtain an adequate idea of the inland commerce, by considering the enormous extent of the inland shipping and the railway facilities of the country.

But it is with the social aspect of American commerce that we [are concerned with] at the present time. The grand business center of the nation is New York City. Having direct and constant intercourse with all parts of the world, the nationality of its merchants is as varied as the countries which they represent. Of the native-born merchants the most numerous and successful originated in the New England States, and are distinguished for their intelligence, ability, and elevated personal characteristics. They live in elegant houses and, while surrounded by all the appliances of prosperity and wealth, are not prone to making a greater display than their less fortunate neighbors. They are plain in their manners and hospitable; and if many of them happen to indulge in keeping up fancy residences in the country, the largest proportion are quite content to spend their summer vacations by the seaside, or among the green hills of their native States. They devote themselves to business with ceaseless activity, and are the men who generally take pleasure in expending their surplus capital upon all sorts of benevolent, religious, and educational institutions. A type of merchants, allied to these, is also found in all the other cities of the country.

Next to them come the English, French, and German merchants, who generally deal in the kind of merchandise sent out from their several countries. In their modes of transacting business and of living, they adhere as closely as possible to the customs of their native lands, but with many modifications. The particular men who laid the commercial foundation of New York were from Holland, but their characteristics have been amalgamated with those of the various nationalities which have, latterly, made that city the most cosmopolitan in the country. While a very large trade is carried on between New York and the Oriental nations, the merchants of Boston have long considered themselves the special patrons and friends of the Far East, and that city has always been a noted mart for the commodities of India, China, and Japan, in which particular it is now finding a rival in San Francisco. Its coasting trade is also very extensive, and it is the port whence various manufactures are shipping in immense quantities. The whaling business, which was formerly divided between several cities, is now almost entirely confined to New Bedford; the merchants of that city, like those of Boston, are proud of their descent from what is called the Puritan stock. In Philadelphia, where the coasting trade is almost unparalleled, they have what is called a Quaker element of population, which has always been noted for its integrity in matters of business. But this city is now vying with New York in the cosmopolitan character of its merchants—and in the person of Stephen Girard produced one of the wealthiest and most eminent merchants in America.[1] With regard to Baltimore and Charleston, Mobile and New Orleans, all these places are the natural outlets of the entire Southern half of the United States, and in all of them may be found an abundant supply of merchants from the four quarters of the globe. And corresponding with the cities just named, there are, throughout the interior of the country, very many cities which have grown into centers of trade and commerce with marvellous rapidity. Among them may be mentioned Chicago (whose merchants are now building up a large tea-trade with China, by way of San Francisco), Detroit, Cleveland, St. Louis, and Cincinnati, Louisville, Buffalo, and Pittsburgh, in all of which may be found the principal nationalities of the globe.

THE MERCHANTS

Looking at the commercial classes . . . it is quite impossible to give prominence to any nationality. It would seem as if, after a brief residence in America, the whole mercantile population, with one exception, becomes permeated with the characteristics of the native-born inhabitants. The exception alluded to is the Jewish race. They are found in every city, and almost in every hamlet—always engaged in bartering and selling, and never in producing, and they are pre-eminently a wandering people. With them, the one great end of life would seem to be to make money, but where they settle down to enjoy it has always been a mystery.

In America, as elsewhere, permanent success in business is chiefly dependent upon character. Honest and upright men are sure to command the respect of their neighbors, and when unfortunate, always find their fellow-merchants

---

1. Stephen Girard (1750–1831), an American philanthropist and businessman who developed a worldwide maritime trading fleet. His large purchase of war bonds during the War of 1812 was a significant help to the cash-strapped U.S. government.

ready to assist them. When men of bad repute happen to make fortunes, they generally find it convenient to settle down among strangers [and] enjoy their ill-gotten gains. One of the effects of the late war in this country was to enrich a large number of adventurers and unscrupulous men, who made money by imposing upon the General Government through political intrigues. And it was because of their foolishness in spending their money and putting on airs to which they were not accustomed, that they came to be known by the opprobrious title of *shoddy*, in remembrance of a spurious cloth which some of them palmed off for the use of the army.

But the average American merchant of today is a man who deserves and receives universal respect. He is intelligent, but not addicted to the profits and pleasures of literature. Engaged all day in the excitement of commercial speculation, he has but little time to devote to reading, and improving his mind. He works so hard and so constantly that work becomes a second nature to him, prostrating his energies and making him indifferent to proper recreations. He considers his word as good as his bond, and, to protect his credit, will make the greatest sacrifice of property. He is liberal in his feelings, and gives freely to all objects which have the sanction of his good opinion. He is hospitable, but would prefer to have his wife and daughters attend to the honors of his house and table. When overcome by reverses he takes a new start, changes the character of his business, perhaps, and will not acknowledge himself as overwhelmed, and proves his mettle by attaining final success. Perhaps there is no feature in the character of the American which is so remarkable as their spirit of enterprise. It is indeed wonderful, and is the cause of their success. But it does not follow that this enterprise is all native-born; a portion of it is undoubtedly brought into the country by intelligent men from the leading countries of Europe.

But let us now take a glance at some of the phases of their commercial life, or rather, at the classes of men who transact the mercantile business of the country; and first, as to the shipping merchants. To carry on their business a large capital is required, and as individuals or organized companies, they are generally the leading patrons of the great shipyards. They have vessels built to order, and also buy them in open market; they establish lines of communication between home ports, by the way of lakes and rivers, and between the United States and foreign countries; and they are the men who so frequently obtain valuable contracts from the Government for carrying the mails, as in the case of the Pacific Steamship Company, which receives not less than five hundred thousand dollars for conveying a semi-monthly mail from San Francisco to China and Japan.

One of the most famous of these men is named Cornelius Vanderbilt [1794–1877]. Another class of shipping merchants are those who simply direct or superintend the business for other parties. They are indeed what might be called, more properly, brokers. The wealthiest man who ever lived in the country, John Jacob Astor [1763–1848], and who left about 25,000,000 dollars, was at one time engaged in the shipping business, and made a great deal of money by sending his ships to China; but he was pre-eminently a trader in furs. Then come the importing merchants. They have their agents located in foreign countries, purchase and sell their merchandise only in the bulk, and are the men who give the greatest impetus to the home trade. Some merchants of this class, engaged in trade with the Oriental nations, have followed the same business for nearly a century; many of them, located in New York and Boston, have acquired immense fortunes. It was the son of one of these, James Lenox [1800–1880], who lately made a donation of a million of dollars for the establishment of a Library and Gallery of Art in New York.[2]

With some few of these importers the custom prevails of selling their goods by auction soon after their arrival; and in this manner whole cargoes of tea from China or sugar from the West Indies were sold within the space of half an hour. But this business has well-nigh been absorbed by the class known as brokers. Another important class of merchants are the wholesale dealers or jobbers. They receive their goods in the bulk from the importers, and sell them by the piece or in broken packages. They sell on credit, and usually confine themselves to a particular class or a few classes of goods. One house, for example, will sell only silk goods; another, all sorts of cotton fabrics; another, the several varieties of woolen goods; another, hardware; and others, wooden or fancy goods and groceries of every description. And then there are what are called the retail merchants. They constitute the most numerous class, and are to be found in every city and village of the land. In the larger towns there is no mingling of dry goods and groceries, but, in the hamlets the merchants find it necessary and to their advantage to keep for sale everything that the people can possibly require—from a yard of calico or a piece of ribbon, a paper of buttons or needles, to a pound of tea or coffee, or sugar or shot, or a cake of soap.

It is sometimes the case, however, that the importing, jobbing, and retail trades are carried on by the same firm, and there is one man located in New York City, Alexander T. Stewart [1803–1876], who is reputed to be the wealthiest and most influential merchant of this sort in the world. His establishments are on the most stupendous scale. He employs agents and clerks by the hundred, and his passion for business is so strong that he is among the first, as well as the last, in his daily attendance at his enormous warehouses. This man began his career a poor and friendless boy [from Ireland], and, be-

---

2. In 1895, the Lenox Library and the Astor Library were incorporated into the New York Public Library.

sides building a palace for himself, giving away millions for the comfort of the poor, he is now engaged at an immense outlay in founding a model town in the vicinity of New York.

The commission merchants form another very extensive class of the business men. To carry on their business, less capital is required than for those already named, but it is important that their credit should be unimpeachable. They receive goods or produce from the manufacturers, or farmers, and sell them to the best advantage, receiving for themselves merely a certain percentage on the amount of sales, in the way of commission, for trouble and expenses. With regard to the subordinates, who are employed by the more important merchants, they consist of drummers, who devote their time to hunting up customers; of clerks, who sell goods and keep the books; of porters, who pack the goods and do the manual labor; and of draymen, who carry the merchandise to the vessels, of every description, and to the railway station.

But there are certain other classes of business men in all the commercial marts whose duties are important and whose influence is extensive. First among these are the auctioneers, who sell to the highest bidders, real estate, furniture, books, works of art, and everything, in fact, which the owners desire to turn rapidly into money. Then come the brokers, who usually devote themselves to one commodity, such as cotton or money, tea and coffee, sugar or grain, who have come to be a numerous and useful class, and who sell only by samples, receiving their pay like the commission merchants. They transact the business which was formerly performed by one class of auctioneers. The class of men known as bankers are those who conduct the moneyed institutions of the country, albeit large numbers follow the business on private account, many of whom, in all the leading cities, have acquired immense fortunes. Of these, perhaps the most successful and celebrated is now a retired citizen of Washington, and who, within the last few years, has given away for purposes of charity and culture many millions of dollars. And still another class of the business men who are very numerous and constantly increasing, are known as Insurance men. They are the managers of extensive corporations who insure, in stated sums of money, all kinds of property from fire and marine disasters, as well as the lives of men who desire to secure a competence for their families in the event of death. From the foregoing statements it will be seen that the machinery of commerce is this country is fully organized and very complete.

THE RAILROADS

To fully comprehend the extent and range of the commercial interests, we must now turn our attention to the system of railways as it exists in the United

States. This is a subject which increases in interest and importance every year. In 1860 this system had already reached a development which was justly regarded as amazing. It was the product of but a short time; every mile of road had been built within the recollection of men who had not yet passed middle life, and three-fourths of it all within ten years. Yet there were in operation more than thirty-one thousand miles of road, which, with their equipment, had absorbed of the capital of the country not less than twelve hundred and fifty millions of dollars, or ten per cent of the entire assessed value of property in the United States. There were men, however, who protested that this interest had outgrown the needs of the country, and was the result of speculative and artificial influences; that it diverted capital from more useful employments, and tended to retard the prosperity of the country. Nor have these men changed their opinion. But what a change has taken place in this business! From the official reports we learn that at the commencement of the present year there were railroad lines in operation to the extent of more than fifty-three thousand miles, which, with their equipment, cost nearly twenty-seven hundred millions of dollars, or twenty-two percent of the entire assessed value of property in the country. Of these more than eleven thousand miles have been built within two years, and at an expenditure of four hundred millions of dollars. In other words, the people of America have contributed during the last ten years more than half as much to build railroads as they have paid in taxes for the support of the Government, including the conduct of the war, and are now contributing yearly for the same purpose two-thirds as much as the whole revenue of the national Treasury. The total earnings of these railroads in 1870 were four hundred and fifty millions of dollars, and the gross tonnage transported equalled one hundred and twenty-five millions of tons, having a value of more than *ten thousand millions of dollars.*

Prior to the late war, the American railroads were regarded almost exclusively in their relations to trade, and the comprehensive study of them was the concern only of the economist. But they have now become the centers of many forms of power in the hands of corporations whose management is concentrated, secret, and largely irresponsible. They hold vast accumulations of wealth; employ a large proportion of the scientific and practical ability of the nation; they exert an immense influence on all the markets, and on the social and material welfare of the whole people. They are also the favorite instruments of speculation, and sources of sudden profit; they wield political agencies and parties, in many places, and even dictate to the State Legislatures. They thus connect themselves with society . . . that their growth and influence are becoming an anxious study, not only for the economist and the trader, but for the politician, the statesman, and the moralist. Hitherto, a large part of the capital thus consumed has been borrowed from foreign nations, and the want is not felt in the United States. But it makes part of the debt on which the productive industry of the country must pay the interest. The subject, as it has been well said, thus presents important and difficult questions for discussion. But all men must acknowledge that the rapid progress of this enormous interest is as wonderful as its present magnitude; and it is plain that of the ultimate extent to which the construction of railroads in America will be carried, no estimate can be formed.

Before leaving this subject we must submit a few additional particulars. The average rate of speed with the passenger-trains in America is thirty miles per hour, and the number of cars in each train varies from five to fifteen; while the freight-trains frequently number not less than one hundred cars. The locomotives are far more powerful and much larger than those on English roads, and wood is the common fuel. In front of the engine is generally placed a massive iron grating, called a "cow-catcher," intended to throw off any animal that may be upon the track; and in winter they are supplied with immense plows for the purpose of cutting through the banks of snow. They are supplied with bells as well as steam whistles, to be sounded when starting, or used to give note of coming danger. They are generally managed by three men, one engineer and his assistant, and one fireman. The passenger-cars are large, and have from eight to sixteen wheels; some of them plain and open to all, and others, called palace cars, are very elegantly fitted up, and occupied only by those persons who are willing to pay an extra fare. On all the trains are also to be found such conveniences as "sleeping" and "smoking cars." The men who manage the trains while running, are the "conductors," who collect the tickets; at the end of each car is stationed a brakeman, who helps to regulate the speed; there are also baggage-men; while boys with books or papers, or fruit, are permitted to pass through the trains; and upon those which carry the United States mail, there is always an officer of the General Post-Office Department. Tickets are purchased before entering the cars, and for every piece of baggage a metal check is given, so that a man may travel a thousand miles or more without casting a thought upon his baggage. The rails are made of iron and steel, and single or double tracks are in vogue according to the necessities of the route; and the longest continuous line of railway in America, running from New York City to San Francisco, is 3,200 miles.

THE U.S. TREASURY, BANKS, AND MONEY

As the primary object of commerce is to accumulate money, it is proper that we should conclude this paper with a general survey of the finances of the United States, and of the people to whom their management is intrusted. At the close of the last fiscal year, the debt of the United States amounted to $2,480,672,427; the reduction, since 1866, when it reached the highest amount, having been $292,563,746. The total receipts of the Government were $566,935,818, while the expenditures amounted to $417,433,346, leaving a balance in the Treasury of $149,502,472. The money spent for the civil service was $19,031,283; foreign intercourse, $1,490,776; military establishment, $57,655,675; naval establishment, $21,780,229; collecting customs revenue, $6,237,137; assessing and collecting internal revenue, $7,234,531; light-house establishment, $2,588,300; mint establishment, $1,067,097; Indians, $3,407,938; and pensions, $28,340,202; while the balance was devoted to miscellaneous expenditures.

Turning from the operations of the national Treasury to the banking institutions, we find the following information. The national banks, which are conducted by private enterprise but made perfectly secure by the General Government, number 1,627, and have a capital of $436,478,311. The chartered banks, which are disconnected from the Government, number 1,882, and have a capital of $503,578,000. The private bankers represent about $400,000,000 of capital. And the savings banks are estimated to hold about $195,000,000. The system upon which all these institutions is managed is quite uniform—each having a president and cashier, a board of directors, and as many clerks as may be required. Taken in the aggregate, the bankers of America are as upright and intelligent as any in existence. But no class, from presidents down to common clerks, are so liable to go astray, and therefore it is that the papers have occasionally to chronicle acts of dishonesty among banking men. On the score of success, it is also worth mentioning that the private bankers have at all times led the way in the more important financial negotiations between the United States and foreign countries. And the late rebellion, as well as the preceding war with Mexico, were both greatly indebted to the skill of two men whose names as bankers have passed into history: William W. Corcoran [1798–1888] and Jay Cooke [1821–1905]. Of the various financial institutions, perhaps the most useful and truly American in its character is that known as the savings bank, the primary object of which is to keep in safety the savings of the poorer classes, for the use of which the bank pays a regular interest. Other banks make it their business to lend money for commercial purposes, but not so with the savings banks, which have more to do with real estate in making use of their funds.

With regard to the circulating medium of the United States, we may remark that it is divided into paper money and specie. The former, which is also called currency, is all issued indirectly from the national Treasury in denominations ranging from ten cents to $1,000, and $356,000,000 being a legal tender, while all the issues under one dollar are called fractional currency. The specie of the country is coined at a national mint, located in Philadelphia, and of course under the direction of the Treasury, and is composed of nickel, copper, silver, and gold; the copper forming one and two cent pieces; the silver, five, ten, twenty-five, and fifty cent pieces; and the gold, one, three, five, ten, twenty, and fifty dollar pieces; to all of which may be added what is called gold and silver bullion. There are also branch mints in operation at San Francisco, Denver, Charlotte, Carson City, and an assay office in New York. While it is true that in all parts of the world money is considered a great power, there is probably no country where the people are so universally imbued with the love of gain, or place so high an estimate on the possession of wealth as is the case in the United States of America.

Chapter Four

Life among the Mechanics

In no way, perhaps, can the magnitude of the mechanical and artisan interests of America be better realized than by walking through the spacious apartments of the Patent Office in Washington [D.C.], where are to be found over one hundred thousand models of American skill and enterprise. Of these, about five thousand have been deposited within the last three years. It might also be mentioned that the cost of supporting the Patent Office and publishing its records, down to the present time, has been twelve millions of dollars. Fifty thousand applications for patents have been rejected; and no inventions, which are inoperative, frivolous, or mischievous can ever be protected by the Government.

Sixty years ago, the manufactures of the country were valued at $200,000,000. Today they are estimated at $3,000,000,000. While the people who are engaged in this enormous business are also counted by millions, their character is varied and interesting. All labor is respected, but this is especially true of skilled labor. The American mechanics are partial to the higher grades of work, and this has a tendency to elevate them in society. They are ambitious to succeed, but often fail because of their attempting too much. As employers, they are faithful and punctual, and they who work as subordinates seldom have cause to complain. As fellow laborers, they are not always considerate, but offences in that direction grow out of individual dispositions. Their minds are not given to abstract thought, but they are fond of industrial organizations. In dealing with men and things, and in surmounting obstacles, they are wonderfully ingenious; and perhaps their chief intellectual distinction is that of inventors. To use the language of another, their moral qualities are not striking, but generally sound. They are a good-natured people, and treat strangers with kindness. Fairness and honesty prevail among them. Discipline is weak. They respect their institutions and deserve to be called a law-abiding people. Their homes are generally well ordered, and their domestic virtues are above the average among European nations. They are fond of amusements, but perhaps too willing to break through the rules of a wise restraint. Different sections and pursuits, however, bring about different results. What is true of one neighborhood is not always true of another. And of course the inhabitants of the newly-settled regions are not generally as far advanced in culture as those located in the older cities and towns. A single brick or block of stone may give us a faint idea of the house to be built of that material; and in like manner, we may partially become acquainted with the manufacturing population by considering a few of its leading classes, who come under the head of mechanics or artisans.

First, as to the very extensive number of persons engaged in the production of flour and meal—the millers of the country. They are to be found in every part, and the business of transforming the various cereals into flour is carried on by steam-mills, as well as those propelled by water and wind power. The mills which are run by water power are the most numerous, and it is only in a few level districts that the old-fashioned windmill is in vogue. Many of the mills in question are of limited capacity and only intended to grind the grain which is sent to them from the immediate vicinity. But in various parts of the country are located very extensive establishments which send their brands of flour to various quarters of the globe. In these larger mills, which run both day and night and employ two sets of hands, they grind and turn out from three hundred to one thousand barrels of flour in each twenty-four hours. Wheat is always a cash article, and to carry on the business a large capital is required. Besides the regular millers and their immediate assistants, these establishments give employment to large numbers of coopers, who manufacture the barrels that are used; but within the past year, complaints have been made against these millers that they were in the habit of using old barrels, which had been used for other purposes. This kind of dishonesty, however, is not common, and will undoubtedly be remedied. The weight of a barrel of flour is always one hundred and ninety-six pounds, and it is universally inspected by a public officer before shipment from the place of its manufacture. The several classes through whose hands each barrel of flour is obliged to pass are the proprietors, the millers and their assistants, the coopers, the inspectors, and finally the book-keeping and shipping clerks. In the larger mills, moreover, regular millwrights are also permanently employed.

Excepting agriculture, there is no branch of American industry which gives employment to so many people as that of boot and shoe manufacturing. The New England States take the lead in this business, and Massachusetts is in advance of all the other individual States, [with] the largest single establishment in that State giving employment to fourteen hundred persons and paying out, in the way of wages, nearly one hundred thousand dollars per annum. And it is reported of one town that it turned out, in one year, boots and shoes enough to amount to five millions of dollars. The States of New York and Pennsylvania come next to New England, and it is estimated that the product of the whole United States is very much more than one hundred millions of dollars per annum, while the raw material in the way of leather has reached a similar amount.

The finer qualities of boots and shoes are usually made in the cities, and chiefly by Germans, and the more ordinary varieties in the country town and villages. In some of these, almost every house has attached to it a shop for making shoes, and all the members of the family, when not engaged in household affairs, or in cultivating a garden, take part in the manufacture. Within the last year, quite a colony of Chinese shoemakers have found employment in New England, and every inducement is given to encourage their coming in greater numbers.[1] Where the sewing-machine is employed, large numbers of shoes are turned out by some families, which are paid for on being delivered to the local dealers, who ship them to the wholesale merchants in the cities. A large proportion of the shoes made are fastened on the bottom by wooden pegs, thereby creating peg factories, in many of which shoe-lasts are made, the combined business amounting to many hundred thousand dollars. About one-third of the people engaged in making shoes are women, and it is said that the aggregate amount now paid to the shoemakers as wages is not far from fifty millions of dollars. With regard to the leather used in this enormous business, it is chiefly manufactured in the country, and its annual production reaches very nearly one hundred millions of dollars.

The manufacture of clothing for men, boys, women, and children has become a business, of late years, of great magnitude. It is confined chiefly to the large cities, and gives direct employment to nearly one hundred and fifty thousand hands, the largest proportion of whom are women. According to the latest published returns of the Census Office, they received in one year nearly twenty millions of dollars in wages, and produced merchandise which sold for about ninety millions of dollars. The general distribution of wealth in America enables the people of all classes to be comfortably and respectably attired, and it is seldom that one class is compelled to wear the cast-off clothing of another class. Out of this fact has grown the vast demand for ready-made clothing of moderate cost, which has developed into an immense and growing trade, giving employment to multitudes of women in the larger

---

1. In June 1870, a large group of Chinese laborers arrived in North Adams, Massachusetts, to work at the Model Shoe Factory owned by Calvin Sampson. This received a great deal of press attention because it was one of the first instances of Chinese factory laborers on the East Coast of the United States. More Chinese laborers would come to work in factories on the East Coast soon afterwards.

cities, who would otherwise find it difficult to support themselves in comfort. The cutters of common clothing are principally Americans, while the Germans and Irish are chiefly employed in the other branches of the business. The wages, both for men and women, are larger than those paid in Europe. The American women are noted for their fondness for dress, and carry the custom of clothing their children to a preposterous extent, and hence the demand for fancy articles of dress is probably greater than in any other civilized country on the globe. And while that wonderful invention called the sewing-machine has not only greatly increased the means of producing, it has at the same time created an increased demand for every variety of clothing.

Of the class of artisans who are engaged in the manufacture of machines, the number is not far from fifty thousand. The machines made by them are well-nigh countless in numbers and variety, ranging from steam-engines and locomotives down to printing-presses and sewing-machines. There is no country in the world where hydraulic machinery or watermills are so abundant as in America, and its water power is practically unlimited. Taken as a whole, the machinists of the country are noted for their superior intelligence, and turn their attention more to what is useful than to what is ornamental. Among the articles which they produce of special importance may be mentioned clocks and watches, firearms, cabinet furniture, cutlery, and all sorts of implements and tools, musical instruments, including organs and piano-fortes, carriages, soap and candles, bricks, tobacco in all shapes, with articles of unnumbered varieties made of iron, copper, brass, glass, and wood. Within the bounds of the Republic may be found the raw material for almost every branch of manufacturing industry. The intellectual power and skill of the American mechanic may be partly appreciated by the fact that the manufactures of the country, when last officially published, numbered one hundred and forty-one thousand, besides the machine-shops of great value and capacity, yielding products to the value of two thousand millions of dollars. These immense results, which include the products of the cotton and wool manufactures, whilst measurably affected by the wealth of the soil and its successful cultivation, are yet traceable to the artisan skill, energies, and industry of the American people. It has been said that the manufacturing and mechanical capacities of the Northern States of America were the primary cause of their success in the late rebellion, and that a more striking illustration of the power and value of such resources is not to be found in history. . . .

Let us now take a glance at the subject of compensation. Common laborers in America earn from one to two dollars per day, without board. The wages for skilled labor are considerably higher, but they cannot be precisely specified, because of the workmen make their own contracts with their employers, the prices being regulated by ability, the season, and the nature of the business. By way of illustration, however, we append the following selection, as about the rate of full monthly wages in vogue at the present time: bakers, fourteen dollars; blacksmiths, ninety dollars; bricklayers, one hundred and twelve dollars; book-binders, eighteen dollars; butchers, twenty dollars; cabinet-makers, ninety dollars; carpenters, one hundred and twelve dollars; cigar-makers, sixty dollars; confectioners, forty dollars; coopers, one hundred dollars; engineers, ninety-two dollars; painters, sixty dollars; printers, ninety-two dollars; harness and saddle makers, sixty dollars; shoe-makers, sixty dollars; tailors, eighty dollars; stone-cutters, one hundred and twelve dollars; watchmakers, eighty dollars; wheelwrights, eighty-four dollars; wagon-makers, ninety-two dollars; spinners and weavers, forty-eight dollars; and wood-carvers, eighty dollars. The above are only about one-fourth of the trades followed in America, but they are among the most important. Generally speaking, the lowest wages are paid in the cities along the Atlantic seaboard, and they increase as the immigrant passes westward, reaching their highest point on the Pacific.

We come now to speak of some of the incidental circumstances connected with that portion of the laboring population devoted to mechanical employments. The hours for beginning and ending a day's work vary according to the seasons of the year. Hitherto, it has been customary to labor ten hours, but this has generally been regulated by agreements between the employer and his hired men. Within the last two years . . . this business has been mixed up with politics, and Congress has been induced to pass a law limiting a day's labor to eight hours so far as the public service is concerned. Whether these regulations have resulted to the advantage of the employed or the employer is not yet settled. It is alleged that they have tended to make discord in the more important establishments, causing the employers to lower the wages paid, and at the same time making the employed restless and more disposed than formerly to demand unreasonable terms.

Looking at the mechanics of the United States in the aggregate, it may safely be said that they live in comfortable houses, have the best of plain food, husband their money with care, and are less addicted to intemperance than are certain classes who think themselves their superiors. They are not so driven in their employments that they cannot enjoy a suitable amount of recreation, and their amusements or entertainments differ according to their nationalities. If the Germans have their gardens, where they congregate at stated times to play games and drink beer; the Irish have their festivals in honor of their patron-saints, as well as their wakes or hilarious funerals; while the native-born inhabitants amuse themselves with pastimes peculiarly American, including picnics, steamboat excursions, and athletic games—but seldom omitting to read the daily papers, or have something to do with politics.

It is true that there may here and there be found artisans who have a hard struggle to get along comfortably, yet a large proportion who are industrious and frugal succeed in laying up money and surrounding themselves with the elegances of life. Indeed, in many parts of the country very marked changes are going on among the people, and successful mechanics are pushing aside the older and more aristocratic families, and giving tone to society. If called upon to say from what sphere the largest number of moderately wealthy men have arisen, our observation would incline us to answer, the mechanical and artisan classes. There are men in all the larger cities, who were once engaged in the most ordinary employments, but who have amassed fortunes that are truly regal, and who are using their wealth in helping the poor, building hospitals, and founding institutions of learning, thereby proving that all the wisdom and benevolence are not possessed alone by the cultivated and intellectual classes.

By way of illustrating the wonderful changes that have taken place in mechanical employment, through the inventions of machinery, we may direct attention to the simple affair called a button. The first manufacturer in America of these useful articles was one Samuel Williston [1795–1874]. He was a country merchant, and while selling buttons made of wood, he conceived the idea of covering them with cloth, and he invented a machine for that purpose, which was the first one invented in the United States. From this humble beginning sprang up a factory, until this man was found to be making one-half of the buttons made in the whole world. Several factories which he established are coining wealth for their proprietors, and are known to the dealers in all climes. This man Williston is now nearly eighty years of age, and is worth about five millions of dollars. He is also a very liberal man, and has endowed several institutions of learning with more than a million of dollars, one of them being Amherst College, where several Japanese students are at the present time receiving their education.[2] The inventive talent of the Americans is universally recognized, and its special power is derived from the existing facilities for education.

. . . The total number of laboring men, women, and children in the United States has been estimated at thirteen (13,000,000) millions; and it is said that the steam machinery of the country is equal to two millions, 2,000,000 of horse-power, or twenty-eight millions (28,000,000) of grown men; so that while one-third of this work is done by laboring men, two-thirds are performed by laboring machines. According to the opinion of a leading British

---

2. In 1870 and 1871, there was only one Japanese student at Amherst College, Niijima Jo (known to his American friends as Joseph Neesima). However, there were several Japanese students attending Rutgers College at this time.

statesman, there are few countries in which the workingman is held in such repute as in the United States. The laboring classes may be said to embrace the entire American nation. American artisans prefer those occupations in which the exercise of brain is in greater demand than that of the elbow, and their chief ambition is to attain the positions of master-workmen. Being educated, they perform their duty with less supervision than is required when dependence is to be placed upon uneducated hands. It rarely happens that a workman who possesses superior skill in his craft is disqualified to take the responsible position of superintendent by the want of education and general knowledge. The true mechanic toils at his trade under the conviction that manual labor, to be effective, must adapt itself almost wholly to the direction of science; and that under that direction, unskilled labor necessarily becomes skilled, and limited trusts enlarge into influential responsibility.

As already [mentioned], the records of the Patent Office bear witness to the effects of general education in the development of mechanical ingenuity in the American people. Nowhere in the world, it has been justly said, does it exist to the same extent. And yet, in some of the most important departments of manufacture, the people are now nearly stationary, while in others they make but little progress. A few years ago, Germany sent to Massachusetts for machinery to manufacture woolen cloth; but today there is scarcely any broadcloth made in any of the United States. Many of the most important improvements in the cotton manufacture are of American origin; and yet the amount of cotton-wool now consumed hardly exceeds that which was required eight years ago. The same is true of various other articles of manufacture. In the last ten years the population has increased about nine millions; and yet the number of persons engaged in many of the manufacturing establishments is not now greater than it was then. The whole increase, therefore, is forced into agriculture and trade; and a new class of men, called "middlemen"—who neither produce, nor sell at their risk—has sprung into existence, who influence upon the prosperity of the country is thought to be of doubtful character.

Chapter Five

Religious Life and Institutions

Under this head we propose to submit a general account of religion in the United States.

There is no state religion, and the Government undertakes only to maintain order and administer justice to all, and they are entirely free to choose any kind of religion, save those which are contrary to its civil laws. Men associate themselves, according to their preferences, under separate organizations called churches. They all believe in one eternal and incomprehensible Deity, and in the immortality of the soul.

All these churches have a book called the Bible. This book is believed to be a revelation from the Deity, or God, and is divided into the Old and New Testaments, the former being called the Hebrew Scriptures and the latter the Greek Scriptures. They claim that the Old Testament contains the most ancient writings known and gives a history of the world and of man from the creation, and also prophesies the coming of Christ at a given time, which is fulfilled in the New Testament, wherein there is a history of the birth and ministry, death and resurrection of Christ, contained in its principal portion called the gospels, the meaning of which word is "good news," and is applied to the story of Christ. Christ is believed to have been "God manifest in the flesh," and all who believe in Him are called Christians.

THE BIBLE

As specimens of each of these parts of the Bible, we quote here some of its leading features. From the Old, the "Decalogue," containing the Ten Commandments or precepts, written on two tables of stone, claimed to have

51

been delivered by God to an inspired man called Moses, at Mount Sinai, in Asia:

And God spake all these words, saying, I am the Lord thy God, which have brought thee out of the land of Egypt, out of the house of bondage.

[1] Thou shalt have no other gods but me.

[2] Thou shalt not make unto thee any graven image, or any likeness of anything that is in the heaven above or in the earth beneath, or that is in the water under the earth; thou shalt not bow down thyself to them nor worship them; for I the Lord thy God am a jealous God, visiting the iniquity of the fathers upon the children unto the third and fourth generation of them that hate me, and showing mercy unto them that love me and keep my commandments.

[3] Thou shalt not take the name of the Lord thy God in vain, for the Lord will not hold him guiltless that taketh His name in vain.

[4] Remember the Sabbath day to keep it holy. Six days shalt thou labor and do all thy work; but the seventh day is the Sabbath of the Lord thy God; in it thou shalt not do any work, thou, nor thy son, nor thy daughter, thy man-servant, nor thy maid-servant, nor thy cattle, nor thy stranger that is within thy gates. For in six days the Lord made heaven and earth, the sea, and all that in them is, and rested the seventh day: wherefore the Lord blessed the seventh day and hallowed. it.

[5] Honor thy father and thy mother: that thy days may be long upon the land which the Lord thy God giveth thee.

[6] Thou shalt not kill.

[7] Thou shalt not commit adultery.

[8] Thou shalt not steal.

[9] Thou shalt not bear false witness against thy neighbor.

[10] Thou shalt not covet thy neighbor's house, thou shalt not covet thy neighbor's wife, nor his man-servant, nor his maid-servant, nor his ox, nor his ass, nor anything that is thy neighbor's. [Exodus 20:1–17]

From the New Testament we quote a part of Christ's Sermon on the Mount, as follows:

Blessed are the poor in spirit, for theirs is the kingdom of heaven.

Blessed are they that mourn; for they shall be comforted.

Blessed are the meek; for they shall inherit the earth.

Blessed are the merciful; for they shall obtain mercy.

Blessed are the pure in heart; for they shall see God.

Blessed are the peace-makers; for they shall be called the children of God.

Blessed are they which are persecuted for righteousness' sake; for theirs is the kingdom of heaven.

Blessed are ye when men shall revile and persecute you, and shall say all manner of evil against you falsely for my sake. [Matthew 5:1–11]

After thus declaring who are blessed, he goes on to say who are the salt of the earth, the light of the world; and that he came to fulfill the law; what it is to kill, commit adultery, and to swear. He exhorts man to suffer wrong; to love even his enemies; to labor after perfectness; to give alms; teaches him how to pray, how to forgive, how to fast, where to lay up treasures, how to serve God and not to serve mammon, not to be careful for worldly things, to seek God's kingdom. He reproves rash judgment, forbids to cast holy things to dogs. He warns them to beware of false prophets; to be doers of the word, and to be like houses built upon a rock. He then teaches the following prayer:

Our Father which art in heaven, hallowed be thy name, Thy kingdom come, Thy will be done in earth as it is in heaven; give us this day our daily bread; and forgive us our debts, as we forgive our debtors, and lead us not into temptation, but deliver us from evil, for thine is the kingdom, and the power, and the glory, forever. Amen. [Matthew 6: 9–13]

In another place he says:

Thou shalt love the Lord thy God with all thy heart, and with all thy soul, and with all thy mind. This is the first and great commandment, and the second is like unto it: Thou shalt love thy neighbor as thyself. On these two commandments hang all the laws and the prophet. [Matthew 22:37–40]

In view of the fact that Christ was crucified on a cross, and the same has ever been considered a symbol of suffering, we quote the following mandate:

And when he had called the people unto him with his disciples, also, he said unto them: Whosoever will come after me let him deny himself, and take up his cross, and follow me. For whosoever will save his life, shall lose it; but whosoever shall lose his life, for my sake, and the gospel's, the same shall save it. For what shall it profit a man, if he shall gain the whole world and lose his own soul? Or what shall a man give in exchange for his soul? Whosoever, therefore, shall be ashamed of me and of my words in this adulterous and sinful generation, of him also shall the Son of Man be ashamed, when he cometh in the glory of his father with the holy angels. [Mark 8:34–38]

What is called the "golden rule" is contained in the following words: "Therefore all things whatsoever ye would that men should do to you, do ye even so to them: for this is the law and the prophets" [Matthew 7:12].

These specimens will show how the Christian religion accords with the Bible.

Both the Old and New Testaments contain, as most of such books do, many wonderful and strange stories, [which are] hard to comprehend. The present writer deems it best not to allude here to any of them, as they appear to him to be of no grave importance in regard to their real religious essence. The increasing influence of the Bible is marvellously great, penetrating everywhere. It carries with it a tremendous power of freedom and justice guided by a combined force of wisdom and goodness.

INSTITUTIONAL INFLUENCE OF CHRISTIANITY

Education, industry, and benevolence are also other strong agents of the Bible influence. The believers in it have schools, and preaching, and missionary enterprises. [And] for the care and help of all the unfortunate they have institutions. These are of three general kinds:

First. Schools for the masses, supported by the State, though this does not exclude schools supported by those directly partaking of the benefit.

Second. Institutions of mercy, asylums for the blind, the deaf and dumb, and the insane. These, because of the great expense attending them, are general, and are supported by the State; while hospitals and infirmaries and lying-in establishments are denominational or belong to churches, and are supported by charitable contributions.

Third. Penal institutions, which include houses of correction for young persons, jail, and penitentiaries. All [of] these being conducted more upon the principle of reforming the evil-doers than upon the principle of punishing them.

THE PROTESTANTS

Having now given a general outline of the system of religion, we will give a few particulars connected with the separate organizations.

There are three great divisions of the Christian Church throughout the world—Protestant, Roman Catholic, and Greek [Orthodox] Church—the latter being organized in the United States only to a limited extent.

The name Protestant was first given in Germany to those who, under the leadership of Martin Luther, an Augustine monk, protested against a decree of Emperor Charles V to support the doctrines of Rome. Pope Leo X had granted indulgences for sins, on the payment of certain sums of money into the church treasury. This was deemed wrong by Luther, who soon founded a religion in opposition to such teachings, and the name Protestant now comprehends chiefly all those Christians who are opposed to the Roman Catholic Church.

Numerous denominations or sects have since sprung up among the Protestants, and they may be named as follows: Methodists, Presbyterians, Congregationalists, Baptists, Episcopalians, Lutherans, Moravians, Quakers, Dutch Reformed Church, Universalists, Unitarians, and a few others. The sacred volume, or Bible, in which all these sects believe, although some of them interpret it different from others, is chiefly printed and circulated by special Bible Societies which, in connection with other Societies established in Europe, have issued the book . . . in one hundred and sixty-five different languages. . . . With regard to the leading principles just mentioned the great multitude of Protestants are agreed. But the sects, in their modes of worship, are somewhat different from each other and must be mentioned separately. Of these, the most extensive class are the Methodists.

This sect was founded in England and is known by the names of Methodist Episcopal and Methodist Connection. It receives its name Methodist from the fact that its members profess to be guided in their living by the methods laid down in the Bible, and the name of Episcopal marks that branch whose power is vested in bishops. They have arranged their doctrines of belief into twenty-five articles, and they recognize the two great sacraments of Baptism and the Lord's Supper, in common with all Protestants. They are ruled by what is termed a Conference, and their principal officers are called bishops, preachers, deacons, and elders. Their churches are plain, and usually built without steeples or towers. Many of the preachers spend their time in travelling from one part of the country to another as missionaries. They own an extensive book establishment, and annually give large sums of money for the support of missionaries in various parts of the world. . . .

Presbyterians are governed by *presbyteries*, or associations of ministers and ruling elders; and several adjoining presbyteries meet under the name of *Synod*. Their *General Assembly*, which is their highest tribunal, is composed of delegates from each presbytery. This body meets annually and attends to the interests of their church throughout the country. Although known in various parts of Europe, this sect was introduced into America from Scotland, where it is the Established Church. The doctrines which they profess are purely evangelical on all points. They give the name of bishop to each minister, and hold them equal in power; the meaning of the word bishop being overseer. . . . The amount contributed and expended for church and missionary operations was about $8,000,000. One of their customs is to have *protracted meetings*, which continue for several days at a time and often terminate in what are called revivals of religion, usually bringing many new members into their congregations.

Closely allied to the above is the sect called Congregationalists. It is the same as that known in England as the Independents, and they have been identified with America ever since 1620, when the Pilgrims first landed on the shores of New England. The essential peculiarity of this church is that it maintains the

independence of each congregation. It is associated with Presbyterians in missionary and publishing enterprises; its colleges are numerous, and its chief
strength lies within the New England States. . . .

Next to the Methodists, in numbers, are the Baptists. They differ from all
other sects in regard to the rite of Baptism. They not only exclude infants from
the rite, but in case of all adults insist upon immersion, or subjecting the entire
body to the influence of water; hence they have in most of their churches a
large tank or basin built behind their pulpits in which the ceremony is performed. However, in some parts of the country it is quite common to perform
the rite in rivers or natural pools of water, and at such times the congregated
spectators help to make the scene impressive. The officiating pastor leads the
person to be baptized into the water, and dips the head under, while pro-
nouncing the necessary form of words. There is a loose dress worn on the occasion by the pastor and the person to be baptized. They do not use the title of
bishop, and they recognize no officials higher than pastors and deacons. One
branch of this sect call themselves Close-Communion Baptists, and will not allow members of other denominations to commune with them. Another branch
are called Seventh-Day Baptists, because they consider Saturday—or the seventh day of the week—the true Sabbath. Still another branch are called Free-
Will Baptists, because of their more liberal opinions. . . .

We now come to the Protestant Episcopal Church. It consists of thirty-nine
confederated dioceses under the care of bishops, to whom their priests and
deacons are subordinate. Each bishop has charge of a diocese or circuit,
which is the extent of his jurisdiction and generally comprises one State.
These representative bishops meet in a General convention, composed of the
"House of Bishops," consisting of all the diocesan and missionary bishops,
and of the "House of Clerical and Lay Deputies," consisting of four laymen
from each diocese. This convention meets triennially. Each diocese has its
Annual Convention, composed of its bishop and assistant bishop, if there be
one, and the priests, deacons, and laity from each congregation; and all dis-
puted questions are referred to the House of Bishops. This sect has a written
form of worship, called a Liturgy, which is embodied in a book called the
"Common Prayer." This book is founded upon the one used by the Church of
England, with such alterations as were deemed expedient upon its adoption in
the United States. There have been several dissensions in this church growing out of the use of this book, and these have caused the division of the sect
into High and Low Church. They are the only Protestants, excepting the
Dutch Reformed, who wear robes or gowns while performing their priestly
office. This gown is of black silk, fitting loosely, and is worn while preaching
and at funerals. A white gown is used for all other services, which is made of
white muslin; bishops wear only the white gown. . . .

The denomination known as Lutherans claims to be more especially Protestant than any other, and takes its name from Martin Luther, although that celebrated reformer was opposed to its use in that connection. Another name for this church is that of the United Evangelical Church. They believe in the actual salvation of infants, dying unbaptized. In other respects the Lutherans substantially agree with all the denominations hitherto mentioned. . . .

Closely allied to the sects already mentioned are those known as the Dutch Reformed and the Moravians. The first of these has its seat of power in New York. . . . The Moravians, though not numerous, have also been noted for their devotion to missionary labor, especially in the northern parts of North America.

All the denominations described above are commonly styled as Orthodox or Evangelical. The following are those which in some degree are in opposition to the others in both faith and principle. They are regarded very liberal and broad in their views.

The sect known as Universalists claim that their doctrines were preached in the United States as far back as one hundred years ago. They reject the doctrine of the Trinity, giving to Christ the second place and making him subordinate to the Father; and while declaring that God is infinite, they believe in the final destruction of evil and the restoration of all human souls through Jesus Christ. They do not believe that any of the human race will be finally lost. Their government is representative and ecclesiastical. . . .

And next come the Unitarians. They oppose the doctrine of the Trinity which is held by the great majority of Protestants, and believe in the absolute unity of God. They do not reject the existence of Christ, but believe him to have been only a man. The manner of their worship is simple and each church manages its own affairs separately. This sect originated in the United States in 1825 and is more popular in Massachusetts than in any other State of the Union. . . . The population connected with this denomination is variously estimated at from fifteen to thirty thousand. Within the last few years they have accepted the cooperation of the Universalists in their efforts to do good; and they have made the following agreement: "Reaffirming our allegiance to the Gospel of Jesus Christ, and to secure the largest unity of the spirit, and the widest practical cooperation, we invite to our fellowship all who wish to be followers of Christ."

CHRISTIAN RITUALS

Having now given a general description of the various Protestant denominations, it is proper that we should be a little more explicit in regard to the sacraments of the Evangelicals. They admit as essential to membership only two sacraments which are considered of Divine institution. These are the rite of Baptism, and the Lord's Supper, called the Communion. Baptism is a representation or seal of the new covenant, and is the appointed ordinance for their introduction into the church, and is a sign of profession, whereby the promises of remission of sins and adoption into the family of Christians are said to be visibly sealed by the Holy Ghost. All the denominations mentioned above, excepting the Baptists, believe in the efficacy of infant baptism, and that it has an influence on all the periods of life. And all administer the rite by sprinkling with water the face of the child or adult believer, and sometimes, as in the Episcopal Church, making the sign of the cross on the forehead while the minister pronounces the words, "I baptize thee in the name of the Father and the Son and the Holy Ghost," showing by these words that the person baptized, or the person bringing the child, believes in the Trinity or True God, the Father as Creator, the Son as Redeemer, and the Holy Ghost as Comforter. The water is used as an emblem of purity, and it is not generally supposed that the outward sign will profit those who live and die without the inward grace, but is to be an adoption into the family of God, by being consecrated to his service, and is a safeguard from evil. . . . Baptism, therefore, is supposed to commemorate the fact that Jesus Christ revealed God to be the Father, himself the Son, and the Spirit the Holy Ghost, or three persons in the one Godhead, all of which are acknowledged by them to exist as a mystery, understood by God alone.

The Holy Communion, or Sacrament of the Lord's Supper, commemorates the fact that Jesus Christ lived and died; and it derived its institution from the fact that, on the evening before his death, he had a supper commonly called the Last Supper, and he gave bread and wine to his disciples, saying, "Take and eat this bread in remembrance of me, and as often as ye drink this cup ye do show forth the Lord's death until He come." These words are found recorded in their Bible, and are believed by all Protestants; so that this Sacrament is revered by all who believe in Christ's sacrifice on the cross to atone for the sins of the whole world. The Episcopalian and the Methodist form of partaking of the Lord's Supper is by kneeling around the chapel in front of the pulpit, while the minister passes before them, first with the bread, which he gives to each one, saying, "the body of our Lord Jesus Christ, which was given for thee, preserve thy body and soul unto everlasting life. Take and eat this in remembrance that Christ died for thee, and feed on him in thy heart by faith, with thanksgiving." He then gives the cup to each one, saying, "The blood of our Lord Jesus Christ, which was shed for thee, preserve thy body and soul unto everlasting life. Drink this in remembrance that Christ's blood was shed for thee, and be thankful."

Right here we may pause for a moment to look at a passage in the New Testament, wherein Christ declares himself to be the bread of life to all believers, and addressing himself to the doubting Jews: "Then Jesus said unto them, "Verily, verily I say unto you, except ye eat the flesh of the Son of man, and drink his blood, he have no life in you. Whoso eateth my flesh, and drinketh my blood, hath eternal life; and I will raise him up at the last day. For my flesh is meat indeed, and my blood is drink indeed. He that eateth my flesh, and drinketh my blood, dwelleth in me, and I in him. As the living Father hath sent me, and I live by the Father; so he that eateth me, even he shall live. This is that bread which came down from heaven; not as your fathers did eat manna, and are dead; he that eateth of this bread shall live forever.'"

The Presbyterians partake of the Sacrament sitting either around a table, which is placed in some churches, or in the pews of the church; the bread and wine being handed to them by the Elders of the church; the minister at the same time repeating words nearly allied to those used by Christ at the Last Supper. The Congregationalists and Baptists use nearly the same forms.

The next rite of importance is that of marriage. It is considered by all Christians to have been ordained by God, and therefore it is a holy rite, not to be engaged in without the sanction of the proper authorities, which make the tie binding and lawful. The ceremony, after a license has been granted, is performed either in the church or at the home of the bride, always by a clergyman, if one can be procured, but in some cases of emergency it can be solemnized or performed by a justice of the peace. The Episcopalians have a written form contained in their Prayer-Book, and the other denominations use also a set form of words, although every one in conclusion makes use of the Bible text: "Those whom God hath joined together, let no man put asunder," which was the injunction used by Christ at the institution of the ordinance.

The burial service for the dead is also a written form with the Episcopalians and Methodists, and is generally performed at the house of the deceased, but members of the church are frequently buried from the church, where the body is carried, for the purpose of having the burial service performed. It is then borne out of the church by persons selected by the family, called pall-bearers, and followed by the relatives and friends to the grave, which has been previously prepared, and is there committed to the earth by the clergyman, lowered into the grave by the pall-bearers, and the earth thrown upon the coffin, and the grave is then closed.

QUAKERS, SHAKERS, NEW JERUSALEM, MORMONS, AND MILLERITES

There are some other religious classes that must be mentioned, who are noted for their peculiarities.

The sect called Quakers or Friends was founded in England by a man named George Fox [1624–1691], and the recognized head in the United States was William Penn [1644–1718]. The epithet Quaker was given to them because they often trembled under an awful sense of the infinite purity and majesty of God. While professing to be guided by the Protestant Bible, they have the following peculiarities: They are very plain in their manner of dress, and in their church buildings; have no special reverence for the Christian Sabbath; speak in public assemblies only when prompted by the Spirit; and they allow women to speak at their meetings. They are to some extent Unitarians in belief, have always been opposed to slavery, and also to war, and never participate in military affairs. The city of Philadelphia was founded by them, and Pennsylvania and New York have been their principal fields of labor. Of late years, they have increased in numbers in the Western States of the Union, and the sect now claims about one hundred and thirty-five thousand members, while they have four colleges, and quite a number of large boarding-schools. As a consequence of a division that once took place among them, a portion of them followed the lead of a man named Elias Hicks [1748–1830], and became known as Hicksites.

The people called Shakers originated in England about one hundred years ago, but are now confined to the United States.[1] The order was founded by two women named Ann Lee [1736–1784] and Jane Wardley [17?–17?], the former having professed to receive Divine light directly from heaven. They believe that God is dual, there being an eternal Father and Mother in the Deity; and the same of Christ. They are ascetics; live in secluded communities; take no part in earthly governments, and are virtually opposed to the marriage relation. They look upon idleness as sin, and are noted for their neatness and plainness of dress. There are twelve societies or settlements of them in the United States, and they have not increased in numbers in the last fifty years, their total number being less than two thousand. They are famous for their knowledge of gardening, and in their principal community, called Mount Lebanon, in New York, which they own in common, they carry on an extensive business in the way of selling seeds and certain articles of domestic manufacture, often yielding an annual income of fifty thousand dollars. In their religious services they frequently resort to dancing, and they believe that their members have the power of healing diseases by means of prayer and abstinence from food.

Another class of religionists are called the New Jerusalem Church, and was originated by Emanuel Swedenborg of Sweden, whose name it sometimes bears. Its doctrines are founded upon the Bible, but are considered by Protes-

---

1. The formal name of the Shakers is the United Society of Believers.

tants as very symbolical. Its followers in America are not numerous, but [are] generally cultured people. Another sect is known as Mormon, whose founder was Joseph Smith, and whose disciples have built up a city in Utah. They are advocates of polygamy, which they practise to a large extent, and Brigham Young is the name of their present leader, but who [recently] has been prosecuted by the General Government as an offender against the criminal laws of the country.

Next come the Millerites or Second Adventists, founded by one William Miller, who preached that the world was to be destroyed on a particular day, when his disciples dressed themselves in white robes and waited for the great event in open fields.[2] Although the predictions of this pretended prophet were not fulfilled, the sect still survives to a small extent. And then there are the Tunkers or Harmless People, who profess to be animated in their religion by fraternal love; the Spiritualists, so called, who boast that they are infidels and heretics; the Perfectionists, who advocate a new and perfect way of society; the Socialists, the Fourierites, the Trappists, who believe in a "community of goods," and finally the Female Seers, who claim that women are superior to men, and that some of their sect have been ordained to be prophetesses and seers.

THE CATHOLICS

The Roman Catholic Church comprises that society of Christians who members acknowledge the Pope as the visible head of the church. Its followers claim it to be coeval with the commencement of the Christian era, although it does not appear to have been fully organized until the fourth century. The Pope is also called a sovereign Pontiff, and the word pontificate is used to denote the reign of a pope. He resides in Rome, and his power extends over all his followers wherever they may exist, and all the churches of this sect in the world are under his supervision. All rules for government and discipline emanate from him, and he is supposed by them to be the present representative of St. Peter, one of Christ's apostles, from whom the popes have in a successive line proceeded. . . . After the Pope, the next in order of rank or power is the archbishop, who presides over the bishops of the dioceses over which he has jurisdiction; then follow the bishops, priests, deacons, and sub-deacons, with similar powers to those mentioned in the Episcopal Church.

What chiefly distinguishes Roman Catholics from Protestants is their belief in the Virgin Mary as an intercessor between God and man, and also in the intercession of the saints or the good persons who have died, and are supposed

---

2. The day that William Miller predicted the Earth would be destroyed was October 22, 1844.

to be in the enjoyment of heaven. These, they think, can hear and transmit the prayers of the faithful on earth to Christ, and that their prayers to the Virgin Mary are especially efficacious with her son, Jesus Christ. They believe in the use of images and relics of saints and the Virgin, and generally wear these and the crucifix, or image of Christ, about their person, as a supposed safeguard from evil, and as reminders of their dependence upon these persons for salvation.

Roman Catholics also believe in the prayers of the church for the dead, and what is called High Mass is said in the church, after death. These prayers are said for the dead, believing that there is a middle state, called Purgatory, between Heaven and Hell, into which persons pass for purification before entering Heaven. Therefore the prayers of the church, and good people, will avail to get them from the transition state into Heaven. Their chief reliance for salvation is in the blood of Christ, but they believe that their good works of prayer, fasting, and almsgiving are meritorious. They believe in the saving grace of Baptism, and that after the form has been used, the person is regenerated, and delivered from all sin. . . .

They believe in the sacraments of confirmation, marriage, penance, extreme unction, and holy orders, but that of the Lord's Supper, or Eucharist, as they call it, and Baptism, are the only ones held in common with Protestants, and we will only give these to show how they differ from that body of Christians. They believe in the Real Presence of the body and blood of Christ in the Lord's Supper; [in other words] that the bread and wine are changed by the consecration of the priest into the real body and blood of Christ. This [is called] Transubstantiation, or the change of the substance from bread and wine into flesh and blood. In performing this sacrament the priest blesses the bread, or wafer, as they call it, and then the people go up to the rail before the altar and kneel down, holding a towel, or white cloth, before their breasts, so that if a particle of the bread should fall it may be received into the towel and not fall to the ground. Then the priest distributes it to them, making the sign of the cross with the consecrated bread upon each one, saying, "The body of our Lord Jesus Christ preserve thy soul unto everlasting life." They do not give the cup to the people, but the priest takes all the wine, believing that after consecration, the whole body and blood and divinity is substantially contained in the wafer or in the wine, and that it is not necessary to give both, and the bread is distributed instead of the wine, as there is danger of spilling the blood of Christ if all receive the cup.

Their church service is called the Mass, and it is in the form of a liturgy or manual. It is read in Latin, that being the original language in which it was written, and the translation accompanies each part, and is thus comprehended by those who can read, while the ignorant accept the form and hear it in a devout manner, believing in the power of the priest to present it to God for them although they may not understand the words. Their faith in the priesthood is extreme, and they have frequent access to them for spiritual advice. The special guide of each individual is the priest who presides over the congregation of which he is a member, and according to his dictation are performed outward acts of contrition, satisfaction, and confession, called penances, by which those sins into which they may have fallen after Baptism can be remitted. Some of these penances are very severe, sometimes requiring much bodily suffering and great sacrifices of time and pleasure, and often much fasting before absolution is given by the priest. They have what is called the confessional, and the apartments devoted to this purpose are small closets or curtained places in the church or chapel, wherein the priest stands, outside of which the person who confesses kneels with head covered, and repeats his sins, and receives the admonitions of the priest. It is not necessary that the individual be known personally to the priest, all that the priest is required to do is to hear and absolve as he may deem proper. This constitutes one great hold which the priesthood have upon the people, and they are willing to accept from them all advice upon matters of conscience. The priests wear robes and vestments while officiating in the church, and these are sometimes very elaborately embroidered and enriched by lace and other materials. This sect denounces as heretics all who do not believe in their teachings, and they believe that none can be saved outside of their church, excepting by a special providence of God, in cases of ignorance of their doctrines.

The Bible is interpreted by their priests for the people, and Roman Catholics are said to be opposed to the free schools of America because the Bible is permitted to be read and taught in these schools. They exclude it from their own schools, as a whole, believing it to be wrong to place it in the hands of those who may be led to interpret it for themselves. That portion of it which they allow for general use contains only the New Testament; the Old Testament being given in the form of a Bible History which has been compiled for this purpose. This question has caused a great deal of discussion in the political world, as free schools are a government institution, and it has influenced many political elections throughout the country, when it has been made a test question whether the candidate under consideration would vote for or against free schools. This plan of interpreting the Bible is another bond of union for Romanists, all being made to adopt the interpretation of this church before becoming a member of the same. However, Protestants differ and are divided into sects, just as men will naturally differ on any subject they are allowed to discuss freely. While the Roman Catholics are all united under one head, there is, however, a secret society among them known as Jesuits, whose special object is for its propagation. It was this society, as our readers will remember, who established themselves in Japan in 1549, but who were destroyed or driven from the Empire in 1595. This sect had, in 1870, seven archbishops, forty-five bishops, seven vicars-apostolic, thirty-five hundred and five priests, and . . . three millions three hundred and fifty-four thousand members.

The most devoted people in this denomination think it incumbent upon them to make certain sacrifices of time and service, and voluntarily go into entire seclusion from the world. For this object they have institutions called nunneries, to which the women retire and take certain vows, and live within their enclosures during the remainder of their lives. Of course, these women never marry. There are also monasteries where the men retire from the world and also take the vow of celibacy, which means never to marry. They devote themselves to teaching young men, and there is a college for that purpose connected with most of these institutions, as there are also female academies connected with the nunneries.

JEWS AND JUDAISM

Another class of religious people who occupy a position peculiar to themselves, are the Jews or Israelites, whose history is identified with ancient and modern times, and more replete with incidents than any other. Although unable to give the extent of their population in America, we may safely state that they are to be found in almost every city and town in the country, and they claim to have about two hundred congregations. Though standing alone in their religious beliefs, they have the credit of manifesting great energy in prosecuting works of charity in behalf of the sick, the needy, and the widows and orphans of their own people. A large proportion of them are wedded to the doctrines of their illustrious father, the patriarch Abraham, with whom the recognition of One Supreme Being originated, and has been cherished to the present day by Bible believers. A party has sprung up among them, of late years, called the Reformed or Christian Jews, and they advocate a religion of progress, in which they have been somewhat successful. They never intermarry with people not of their own race, and from time immemorial have been noted for their sagacity in accumulating money. Their history, which occupies a large space in the Bible, is considered the most wonderful in the annals of religion throughout the world.

Of all the rites or ceremonies which are practiced by the Jews, the most strict and solemn is that which annually occurs on what they call the Day of Atonement [Yom Kippur]. It is marked by a rigid fast, which commences at sunset on one evening, and ends with sunset on the following day, during which time the more faithful of the sect will not permit a morsel of food or water to pass their lips. During all this period they offer up prayers, clad in such garments as are used in burying the dead; and until the close of this special season for religious worship their synagogues are crowded with worshippers, who, like the Quakers, invariably wear their hats in all public assemblies.

RELIGIOUS INSTITUTIONS

In looking at the people of the United States in the aggregate, it has been estimated that about seven-eighths of them are either allied to the Protestants, have no religion at all, or come under the head of miscellaneous sects, while the remainder are Roman Catholics. Nearly all the denominations are amply supplied with theological institutions, which number more than one hundred, and those who are educated in them are always expected to become the advocates of the doctrines in which they have been instructed.

As to the benevolent institutions for the relief of suffering humanity, they are to be found in nearly all the individual States, and are chiefly supported by the Protestant sects, or by the people, through their legislatures. In their internal arrangements all these asylums and hospitals are in keeping with the advanced improvements of the age. By means of raised letters the blind are enabled to read; by wise treatment the insane are made docile, and contented with their unhappy condition; and by personal kindness and sign-alphabets the deaf and the dumb are instructed and made to forget their misfortunes. The total number of these unfortunates in the United States is nearly one hundred thousand.

To give an account of the hospitals, the homes for the orphan and widow, and other charitable institutions of the country, would occupy more space than can be afforded in this work, but we can state that they are very numerous, liberally endowed, and as efficiently conducted as any in the world. When necessary, people from every clime can find a convenient place where they may be cared for, whether their troubles are the result of poverty, of accidents, of sickness, or any other misfortunes.

Of all the visible evidences of prosperity among the religious people of America, the most impressive and extensive are the churches or temples of Christian worship. Not only are they to be found on almost every street in the larger cities, but they are the leading architectural attractions in the towns and villages of the whole country. Bricks and every variety of stone are employed in their construction. Every school of architecture is called upon to beautify them with their designs, and the money expended in building them ranges from ten or twenty thousand to one or two millions of dollars. The current expenses of these churches are paid by voluntary subscription, or with the money received through the renting or sale of pews or seats.

The ministers who preside over these churches, excepting the Roman Catholics, who are supported in a different manner, receive by way of compensation from five hundred to ten thousand dollars, according to the wealth of the congregations. These churches are open for public worship twice on every Sunday, and occasionally on weekday, and are never used for mere secular purposes. In many of these churches, elaborate music, consisting of singing combined with magnificent organs, forms an important part of the services. It is from these churches, moreover, that the money goes forth for the support of charitable and benevolent institutions, and for spreading the religion of the Bible by means of missionaries throughout the world. There is also attached to most of these congregations what are called Sunday Schools, in which children, both rich and poor, are instructed in the ways of Christianity. While it is true . . . that there is no State religion in America, it is also true, however, that the religious denominations of the country occasionally exercise a decided influence in public affairs. [For example], when a man of mark puts himself forward as a candidate for an elective office, his chances of success very frequently turn upon the nature of his religious belief. Hence we find a perpetual warfare going on in America between the Protestants and Roman Catholics, which is anything but creditable to the parties, an honor to the country, or a blessing to the world.

FREE MASONS AND ODD FELLOWS

Although only indirectly connected with the foregoing subject, we deem it quite proper to append in this place a few words in regard to the noted secret societies known as Free-Masons and Odd-Fellows. The first, which is identified with the history of architecture, is claimed to have originated in the religious mysteries of the ancient world—and especially in Asia Minor. Members of the fraternity are found in every quarter of the globe, but it is perhaps more flourishing in the United States than elsewhere. They have what they call a Grand Lodge in all the States of the Union, and many of the most distinguished men in this country have been members of the Order. Their highest officer is called a Royal Arch Mason. In the exercise of charity, particularly towards their fellow-members, they are eminently liberal; and their houses, which are called temples, are numerous, and often very handsome; and their publications are highly respectable, if not abundant.

The fraternity known as Odd-Fellows bears a general resemblance to the Free-Masons, traces its origin to the fourth century, and has, until recently, been confined to Great Britain and the United States, in which latter country it is exceedingly prosperous. Like the Free-Masons, they have their Lodges and many officers, and it is said that in the last forty years they have expended for charitable purposes not less than fifteen millions of dollars. The relief furnished to its members during sickness, and to their families after death, is accorded to them as a right. Connected with this Order is an institution which they call the Grand Encampment, whose members are known as patriarchs and priests, and which consists of past officers of the several subordinate Encampments. The State Grand Lodges consist of the past officers of the subordinate Lodges; and the Grand Lodge of the United States, which is the highest body of the Order in this country, is formed of Representatives elected by the several State Grand Lodges. Some years ago, by the action of the present Vice-President of the United States, Schuyler Colfax (who is a distinguished member of this Order), women were admitted to a partial fellowship in it; and since then, at stated periods, the different subordinate Lodges confer upon such wives and widows of Odd-Fellows who may desire it, what is termed the "Degree of Rebecca."

THE YMCA

There is one feature connected with religion in America which is peculiar to this country, and must not be forgotten in this summary. We allude to the *Young Men's Christian Associations.* There are one thousand of these societies in the United States, and they are conducted by an active element in the various churches, and without any denominational distinctions. They are supported by the free-will contributions on the part of their members, and their buildings, in the larger cities, are frequently quite splendid and beautiful. They are generally so arranged as to afford, under one roof, a library of the best books, a Reading-Room, supplied with the leading newspapers and periodicals of the day, a General Receiving-Room, where religious services are held for those who wish to attend them, and Lecture-Room, where able men are invited to lecture. To all of these privileges, excepting the lectures, the public are admitted without any charge, and the good which these associations have already accomplished, in elevating the tone of society, is considered in the light of a national blessing.[3]

---

3. For a study of the YMCA in Japan in the late nineteenth and early twentieth centuries, see Jon Thares Davidann, *A World of Crisis and Progress: The American YMCA In Japan, 1890–1930* (Bethlehem, Pa.: Lehigh University Press, 1998).

MY THOUGHTS ON CHRISTIANITY

It is proper, before concluding this chapter, that the writer should submit a few particulars respecting its arrangement, which are somewhat personal to himself. After his return to Japan from Europe [and the United States] some years ago he was frequently questioned by his countrymen as to his opinions about the Christian religion. In his replies, he took the ground that, so far as he could understand it, the Bible was a good and a wise book, but that it contained many things he did not understand. That while the people who called themselves Christians claimed to have the only true religion, and pretended to be better than all other men, they did not, in that particular, differ from the Chinese or Japanese, who assert the same claims for their religions. He thought it advisable that those who desire to form any opinion on Christianity, should acquaint themselves with it by close and attentive study, and then to judge for themselves. Hence, in the present chapter his desire has been simply to give facts, and in the plainest possible terms. Whatever may be his private opinions on matters of such great importance, he has not thought it proper for him either to oppose or advocate them. According to his observations, a very large proportion of the American people are known by the name of Christians, and yet a great many things are said and done by them which do not accord with the principles of their own Bible. But is not this true of every nation upon the earth? Where men think that they know everything, and boast of their superior wisdom, the presumption is that they have yet much to learn. All human experience, as well as the Bible of the Christians, inculcates the idea that before men can be wise and good, they must be humble. It would be a very wonderful thing, should the time ever arrive, when the so-called Christians who profess the faith, but do not live up to it, shall cease to boast of the superiority of their religion, and regard themselves as worse than all other people, because of their guilt in making insincere professions. True Christianity may not be considered as identical with the general sense of civilization—in which the good and the bad participate—but true philosophy would seem to teach that it should be a leading element in such civilization.

[The following two paragraphs were originally at the end of *Life and Resources in America* in a section titled, "Additional Notes."]

After the foregoing . . . on Religious and Educational Life had been printed, we obtained some later official information on those subjects, which we append in this place. In 1870 three States of the Union passed laws compelling the education of all children with sound minds and bodies. The total number of colleges in the country is 368, of which 261 are supported by the different religious denominations. In these institutions there are 2,962 instructors and 49,827 pupils; in 99 of them males and females are instructed, while the balance are confined to males. Besides these, there are 136 institutions for the superior instruction of females alone, in which there are 1,163 teachers and 12,841 pupils. Of medical schools, there are 57; theological schools, 117; law schools, 40; normal schools, 51; and business schools, 84. Connected with these various institutions there are 180 libraries, with 2,355,237 volumes. The benefactions to educational objects by private citizens were quite unparalleled in 1870, amounting in the aggregate to $8,435,990.

With regard to the effect of education upon crime, we find that there was one homicide to every 56,000 people, one to every 4,000 in the Pacific States, and one to every 10,000 in the Southern States. At least 80 percent of the crime of New England is committed by those who have no education; in all parts of the country, 90 percent. Of the criminals [who] were illiterate; 75 percent were foreigners; and from 80 to 90 percent connected their career of crime with intemperance. From these figures, the conclusion is inevitable that ignorance breeds crime, and education is the remedy for the crime that prevails.

Chapter Six

Life in the Factories

The term factory, as employed in America, means a place where men and women are engaged in fabricating goods. In this paper it is proposed to speak of those establishments, especially [those] where the staples of cotton and wool are turned into the woven fabrics commonly known as calicoes, sheetings, carpetings, cloths made of both materials, as well as hosiery and worsted goods, blankets, shawls, table-covers, felted cloths, and bed-spreads.

COTTON AND WOOL PRODUCTION

The largest amount of cotton ever produced in this country in one year was in 1860, the year before the late rebellion, when the figures reached 4,669,770 bales. Each bale weigh[ed] 465 pounds, and the factories numbered 1,091. According to the last published statistics, the supply of cotton reached only 2,500,000 bales; the number of cotton-mills or factories 831, of which 444 are in New England, 86 in the Southern States, 220 in the Middle States, and the balance in the Western States. The total value of the cotton crop was $270,000,000, and it is said that the people producing it sold and exported the whole of it, excepting the value of $10,000,000 kept for home consumption. However we may arrange the cotton statistics of America, the fact remains that its cotton manufactures, though still very large, have declined of late years, and are greatly excelled by those of England. . . .[1]

---

1. During the American Civil War, some cotton mills in the southern states were destroyed by Union forces. A more consequential cause of the drop in cotton production in the United States was that India significantly increased its output of cotton after Britain took control over much of the country following the Sepoy Rebellion of 1857.

As is the case with cotton, the most numerous woolen factories of America are found in New England. With these few particulars in view, we may proceed to speak of the peculiarities of factory life in the United States which, of course, must be done in very general terms.

THE FACTORIES AND THE WORKERS

Wherever in the northern portions of the country is to be found the best supply of water suitable for running machinery, there do the manufacturing establishments mostly congregate. And it is because New England is rocky and not well suited to agriculture, and also because its rivers are numerous and well adapted for mills, that its manufactures have become especially celebrated. The villages which have sprung up out of this kind of business are to be found in every part of the land. While some of [these villages] consist only of the houses collected around one factory, others contain a number of factories and are proportionally large. In one place the ownership may be vested in one man; at another place in an organized company of men. And then again, a single man or family may be the proprietor of several factories, employing thousands of hands to carry them on, and requiring millions of [dollars] for their support. In this connection, a few such men as Amos and Abbot Lawrence and William Sprague have acquired national reputations.[2] In many instances the small villages alluded to are located in the midst of beautiful scenery, and the necessary surroundings of the mills, which give them existence, are pleasant little churches, comfortable school houses, shops for the sale of household merchandise, and appropriate houses for the shelter of the operatives. Men, women, and children are all employed in these factories and, generally speaking, they absorb all the laboring population to be found in the country immediately surrounding them, as well as many persons from abroad. The idea of strict discipline is recognized and carried out, from the overseer down to the humblest workman, and it is in these small villages that a greater amount of comfort is enjoyed by the persons employed than in the larger manufacturing cities. Of course, the facilities for obtaining the raw materials of cotton and wool, and for transporting the manufactured goods to market, are commensurate with the necessities of the case; and the establishments where the goods are sold are generally located in the larger cities.

---

2. Amos Lawrence (1786–1852) and Abbot Lawrence (1792–1855) were brothers who founded A and A Lawrence, a large mercantile house in Boston, Massachusetts. After starting in the retail textile business, they built large cotton and wool cloth mills in a town soon to be named after them, Lawrence, Massachusetts. They also invested in and promoted New England railways. William Sprague (1830–1915), was governor of Rhode Island from 1860–1863 and U.S. senator from 1863–1875. Sprague was also the owner of a very successful calico printing business.

A truly comprehensive idea of factory-life in America cannot be had without considering its character as we find it in the larger towns or cities, and no better example can be selected for that purpose than the city of Lowell, in Massachusetts. What may be said of this place is also true, only in a different degree, of all the factory-towns throughout the country, and especially such places as Lawrence, Providence, Norwich, and Worcester. [I]t may safely be said that the aggregate number of persons who obtain their living by means of the cotton and woolen factories of the country is not less than three hundred thousand. The growth and prosperity of Lowell as a manufacturing town is without many parallel in America. It lies on the river Merrimack, and the water-power is formed by dams that are thirty feet high. It has not less than fifteen manufacturing corporations, with about sixty mills, which employ a capital of fifteen millions of dollars, and support about fifteen thousand hands, from the beginning to close of the year, while the entire population of the city is nearly fifty thousand. All the mills are heated by steam and lighted by gas. The women who work in them far outnumber the men. Although a few years ago a much larger proportion of these [workers] were native Americans, so great a change has taken place in this particular that the majority are now foreigners, and chiefly Irish. The men are without ambition, and the women work for the sole purpose of making money, and not because they like the employment. Widows are there, toiling for the education of their children; and daughters are there, hoarding up their wages to pay the debts of improvident fathers. The labor of the women is essentially on an equality with that of the men; but while the former receive from two to three dollars per week, in addition to their board, the latter receive from four to six dollars for the same period. The time for labor ranges from ten to twelve hours per day, and extra sets of hands are often employed for night-work. The hands are summoned to their work by the ringing of bells. A brief time only is allowed for meals, and the only opportunities which the operatives have for recreation or study are at night, when worn out with the fatigue engendered by the jar and whirl of the machinery in the mills. When the American element prevailed in these factories, an earnest effort was made to elevate the minds of the thousands of girls employed, and for a time these efforts were successful. A monthly periodical was established, called the "Lowell Offering," which was supported entirely by the productions of females working in the mills, and in which many valuable papers were published. For a time this magazine was very successful and excited much wonder and comment among the factory-people of New England, but the novelty soon wore off, and the work was suspended. A leading American writer, while mourning over this fact, and also over the fact that there was so little comfort to be found in these large manufacturing towns, said that the patron-saint of Lowell was *Work*; that the "Factory Girls" might be counted by the acre; that the motto over the gateways should be, "Work or Die"; and that the fifty factories in the city were each larger and more imposing than the temples of worship in Japan and China. In the largest of these mills from one thousand to fifteen hundred women or girls are constantly employed, and from three hundred to five hundred men. Each manufacturing company owns from twenty to thirty dwellings, which are leased to responsible persons as boarding-houses, for the exclusive benefit of the hands employed in the factories. These dwellings are large enough to accommodate from forty to fifty inmates, and the sexes are kept entirely separate. The corporations also provide hospitals in which the work-people find attendance in sickness, for which, if they be unable to pay, the employers are responsible.[3]

While it is true that the young people who are obliged to work in the factories have little or no time to cultivate their minds, the younger children of the married people have every facility afforded them to obtain knowledge. The common schools of [Lowell] are numerous, well conducted, and chiefly under the direction of competent female teachers. There is also a good library in the city, where all who are fond of reading, no matter how poor, can be furnished with useful and entertaining books. The religious privileges are enjoyed by all by means of numerous churches and the weekly day of rest, which is called Sunday, are all that could be desired.

Notwithstanding these many advantages, recent writers on this subject have declared that the extinction of the educated American operative has become an accomplished fact, and the mills of Lowell, as well as those of the Atlantic States generally, are now worked . . . by immigrants from Europe—from Ireland, Wales, and Germany. But these, as they grow in intelligence, and begin to go westward like their predecessors, demand higher wages, shorter hours for work, and more freedom. They have learned the European lesson of fighting employers by combinations [unions]. The problem has become so confused that the manufacturers are beginning to look for relief to the Chinese, a number of whom have already been induced to enter the factories of New England. American girls are said to be growing dissatisfied with the restraints of factory-life, where they have to compete with the more rugged and experienced women from European countries. Hence they go to the larger cities and become domestic servants. But that kind of employment they find irksome, and so they make another effort to succeed according to their wishes, and emigrate, as best they can, to the Western States.

---

3. Within a few years, Japan would have textile mills (cotton and silk) similar to those being discussed in this passage. See Patricia Tsurumi, *Factory Girls: Women in the Thread Mills of Meiji Japan* (Princeton, N.J.: Princeton University Press, 1990).

In the further elucidation of this subject, it is proper that we should consider the opinions of the manufacturers themselves. They assert that the opprobrious epithet of "white slavery," which has sometimes been applied to the labor in the New England factories, is wholly unwarranted. They claim to have purged it of every element of feudalism; that they have avoided the English plan of employing whole families in the mill, often including children, who should have been at school—the families being kept in a state of absolute dependence upon the mill, and exposed to suffering whenever business was not prosperous. They claim also to have abolished the custom of payment by orders on a factory store, which tended to involve the work-people in debt, and they instituted the practice of weekly payment of wages in money. [The manufacturers claim] that they have done all that could be done, to secure the independence as well as comfort of the American operatives.

[Here we] furnish a further illustration of factory-life in America by submitting a brief description of what may be termed a model New England establishment, as follows: It is located in the city of Lawrence; is a joint-stock company, with 150 stockholders and 9 directors; has 100,000 spindles; and has a capital of $2,500,000, while its property is valued at a considerable advance on that sum. The manufactured goods, consisting chiefly of fabrics for the wear of women, made both of cotton and wool, which are annually sold, amounting to about $7,500,000; and the total dividends declared, during the last twelve years, was more than $3,000,000.

The total number of work-people employed in this factory is 3,600, of whom the men number 1,680; women, 1,510; boys between ten and twelve years of age, 80, and between twelve and eighteen, 140; girls between ten and twelve, 40, and between twelve and eighteen, 150. The lowest weekly wages, according to gold rates, are as follows: for men $6.75; women $2.48; boys, $2.85; and young girls, $1.82; while spinners, weavers, and a few others, receive according to the quantity of goods produced, and some of them large wages. Very many of the operatives are frugal with their money and have invested their earnings in the stock of the company itself, deposited it in Savings Banks, or purchased the bonds of the General Government. Some of them have been so successful as to be elected members of the City Government; and not a few are the owners of comfortable houses. Where men are obliged to hire houses, they pay only one-eighth of their wages for rent. And for the comfort and accommodation of the unmarried females a large building has been erected, holding not less than eight hundred persons, who pay for food, lights, and washing, only one-third of their regular wages.[4] Connected with the establishment is what they call

---

4. In other words, these women factory workers are paying one-third of their regular wages back to the company to live in a huge, company-owned dormitory.

a "Relief Society" organized for the care and support of the sick among the work-people. Every possible attention is paid both to the morals and intellectual culture of the operatives. No men are employed who are intemperate in their habits, and the use of profane language and the ill-treatment of subordinates strictly prohibited. All females are compelled to be at their lodgings by ten o'clock at night, and none of them are permitted to attend improper places of resort. No child under ten years of age, according to law, is allowed to work in the factory, and all the boys and girls must be furnished with from eleven to sixteen weeks of schooling in each year, and all the schools are paid for by the company. Of the persons employed, less than fifty in every thousand are unable to read, and for the benefit of all there is a well-conducted library with pleasant reading rooms for both sexes, and every facility is afforded for attending lectures and places of profitable amusement. A week's labor in this establishment will produce more yards of cloth than is produced in any European mill, but it is claimed that a yard of cloth costs less in Europe. . . .

Let us now look for a moment at some of the local results of the cotton and woolen manufactures of recent times. It has been said that where one person a century ago consumed one yard of woven goods, the consumption per head has since risen to about twenty-six yards. This vast difference in the comforts of every family, by the ability which they now possess of easily acquiring warm and healthful clothing, is a clear gain to all society and to every individual as a portion of society. It is more especially a gain . . . to the females and the children of families, whose condition is always degraded when clothing is scanty. The power of procuring cheap clothing for themselves and for their children, has a tendency to raise the condition of females more than any other addition to their stock of comfort. It cultivates habits of cleanliness and decency, which are considered in America great aids to virtue, if not actual virtues themselves. There is little self-respect amid dirt and rags, according to the American belief, and without self-respect there can be no foundation for those qualities which mostly contribute to the good of society. The power of procuring useful clothing at a cheap price has tended to raise the condition of women in America, and the influence of the condition of women upon the welfare of a community can never be too highly estimated. If there be one thing more remarkable than another in the visible condition of the people of the United States it is the universality of good clothing. The distinction between the rich man and the artisan, or between the lady and her maid, is oftentimes almost imperceptible. Perhaps the absence of mere finery, and the taste which accompanies good education constitute the chief difference in the dress of various ranks; and this feature of the present time is a part of the social history of America.

MACHINERY AND INNOVATIONS

The history of the cotton and woolen manufactures has occupied the minds of many of the ablest men in the world, and their developments are of vital interest to the whole human family. The arts of spinning and weaving were slowly developed from the time of the simple distaff, and it was just as they had reached something like completion that an American named Eli Whitney [1765–1825] invented the cotton gin in 1793, which at once gave a new character and impulse to the growth, as well as the manufacture of cotton.[5] This invention was the final step, by which the whole process of manufacturing cotton into cloth was effected by machinery. Just about that time, steam was introduced to the world as an agent of limitless power in driving machinery of every kind. New channels of internal communication were opened between the different parts of the world. Chemistry furnished the means for rapidly bleaching the fabrics produced from cotton, and all the resources of science and skill, of invention and industry, seemed combined to create an immensely increased demand for the raw material upon which all these labors were to be expended. And if something like this enterprise can be transported to Japan, what may we not expect in the future from that Empire?

There are many wonderful inventions connected with the manufacture of cotton, but nothing is perhaps more astonishing than the rapidity with which some portions of the machinery is employed. Notice the fact, for example, that the very finest thread which is used in making lace is passed through the strong flame of a lamp, which burns off the fibers, without burning the thread itself. The velocity with which the thread moves is so great that the motion cannot be perceived. The line of thread, passing off a wheel through the flame, looks as if it were perfectly at rest; and it appears a miracle that it is not burned. The primary object of the extensive and complicated machinery employed in the manufacture of cotton has been, of course, cheapness of production, and in that particular the advance, from the time of the distaff, has been wonderful and success complete. Nor has this been done at the expense of the working classes. Ten years after the introduction of the machines, the people employed in the trade, spinners and weavers, were more than forty times as numerous as when the spinning was done by hand. It was thought that the newly discovered power might supercede human labor altogether; but such was by no means the case. It only gave a new direction to the labor that

---

5. A distaff was a long staff used for holding wool or cotton while the thread was spun. There were different types of cotton gins in use in the United States by the 1790s, of which Eli Whitney's became the most widely known.

had previously been employed at the distaff and spindle, and it increased the quantity of labor altogether employed in the manufacture of cotton at least a hundredfold. What is here said of the machines for manufacturing cotton is also true of those employed in the woolen, the silk, and the linen manufactories, and to the uneducated eye and understanding they are all wonderful, and of incalculable value to the commercial world.

There is another curious machine which we may, with propriety, mention in this place, and that is one for making needles. Hitherto the largest number of needles used in America were made in England. But there is a machine in New Haven in which the whole process is performed without the manual labor of a single person. A coil of steel wire is put into it, then the machine cuts it off at the required lengths, punches the eyeholes, counter-sinks the eyes, and then sharpens the needle, when it drops out a perfected thing. They are also arranged and put up in paper by another machine, and the number of needles thus manufactured per day by each machine is about forty thousand.

Before dismissing the subject under consideration, we would submit to the Japanese reader a few remarks on the art of printing cloth in colors, whose object is merely to beautify the very numerous fabrics which are made in the various factories already alluded to. It applies to the most common as well as to the finest productions of the loom, and the science of the dyer, the beauty of his patterns, and the perfection of his machinery, have become universally celebrated. As an experienced writer has said, there is a striking, although natural parallel, between printing a piece of cloth and printing the sheets of a book or newspaper. Block-printing is the impress of the pattern by hand, as block-books were made four centuries ago.[6] There are no block-books now, for machinery has banished that tedious process. But block-printing is used for costly shawls and velvets, which require to have many colors produced by repeated impressions from blocks covered with different colors. Except for the most expensive fabrics, however, this mode is superceded by block-printing with a press, in which several blocks are set in a frame. Then again they have what they call cylinder-printing, which resembles the rapid working of the book-printing machine, each producing with great cheapness. As the pattern has to be obtained from several cylinders, each having its own color, there is great nicety in the operation, and the most beautiful mechanism is necessary for feeding the cylinder with color, moving the cloth to meet the revolving cylinder and giving to the machine its power of impression. But those who witness this operation can hardly realize the ultimate effect subse-

---

6. Apparently a reference to Johannes Gutenberg and the development of the printing press in Europe in the mid-fifteenth century. However, block printing and movable-type printing were developed in Korea and China centuries earlier.

quently obtained by the process of dyeing. Fast colors are produced by the use in the patterns of substances called mordants, which may be colorless themselves, but receive the color of the dye-bath, which color is only fixed in the parts touched by the mordants, and is washed out from the parts not touched. Other processes are also employed which enhance the beauty of the fabrics.

It is thus seen that the chemist, the machinist, the designer, and the engraver, see the calico-printing works in operation, so that the carrying on of this complicated business can only be profitably done on a large scale. Very numerous also are the employments required merely to produce the dyes with which the calico-printer works. The mineral, vegetable, and even the animal kingdom combine their natural productions in the colors of a lady's dress. There is the sulphur from Sicily, salt from Austria or Turk's Island, peculiar woods from Brazil, indigo from the East and West Indies, madder from France, and insects from Mexico. The discoveries of science, in combination with experience and skill, have set all this industry in motion and given a value to innumerable productions of nature which would otherwise be useless or unemployed. And they also create modes of cultivation which are important sources of national prosperity. But of all the discoveries of chemistry, in this connection, was that of chloride of lime, which has become the universal bleaching powder of modern manufactures. What was formerly the work of eight months is now accomplished in an hour or two so that a bag of raw, dingy cotton may now be converted into the whitest cloth within the space of a single month.

TARIFFS, IMPORTS, AND EXPORTS

As an appropriate conclusion to the foregoing remarks, we may now submit a few general facts on the American Tariff of duties on imported merchandise. This has been the means on which the Federal Government has chiefly depended for its support ever since it came into existence. It has also been amply sufficient for affording money to extend its territory, carry on wars, execute treaties, and accumulate a large property in lands, buildings, and materials for war. From the earliest times, however, the people have been divided into two great political parties on this subject, and yet the friends and opponents of the measure have in the main admitted that it is the best means for raising the public revenue, inasmuch as direct taxation has been thought impolitic for Federal revenue.[7] There is a large class of people, moreover,

---

7. There was no federal income tax in the United States until 1913.

who believe that the levying of duties is detrimental to the agricultural interests. These, and numerous questions of a similar character, have long occupied the minds of the leading statesmen of the United States, and they remain unsettled to this day. As the political parties have gained ascendency, so have the tariff rates been changed or modified, from time to time. In looking back over the forty years prior to the late Civil War, we find that the rates of duty have varied from eighteen to forty-eight per cent. . . . [Imports, exports, and tariffs] have an important bearing upon the success, or want of success, of the factory system in the United States, and this is apparent to all men who investigate these subjects.

In accounting for the excess of imports over the exports, it may be stated that the difference arises chiefly from the importation of articles of luxury. The American people are practical, and while they confine themselves chiefly to producing the necessaries and comforts of life, and to accumulating money, they are quite willing to obtain their fashions and articles of luxury from Europe. Notwithstanding the immense immigration from abroad, the American people have always had enough to feed all who come to their shores, and to provide employment for all. The strength of the nation is shown by the fact that, in spite of the large amounts which are expended for the mere elegancies of life, which the rich bring over from Europe, the country is constantly prospering.

Statistics show that the trade of the United States has been regularly progressing, until interfered with by the late Civil War. Generally speaking, the exports have exceeded the imports, and the balance of trade has been in favor of America. The export of grain does not depend upon the state of the crops so much as upon the wants of other countries. The great variety of the native productions exported gives assurance of the impossibility of failure of the resources of the nation. Figures also show that there is no industrial pursuit in which the people of the United States do not regularly progress, and that there is little demand for any class of produce which they are not able to supply.

As the revenue of the country depends in a great measure upon the customs duties, so does its prosperity chiefly depend upon the amount of its exports of bread-stuffs and all sorts of merchandise. Yet, as the theories which have been brought to bear upon this subject are widely different, and have occupied the minds of the ablest writers, they cannot be entered upon in this chapter. Upon one subject, however, all men are agreed: that the extension of commerce will do more than anything else to diffuse the blessings of civilization, to bind together the universal society of nations, by sharpening and at the same time gratifying their mutual wants and desires, and to maintain undisturbed that tranquility so indispensable to its full development.

[As a postscript, Mori added a list of wages, prices, and agricultural re-sources he had just received from the United States Bureau of Statistics and the Census Bureau. As he had already discussed similar statistics previously in this chapter, this postscript has been omitted. For those who are interested, see United States Department of the Interior, *Ninth Census of the United States, the Statistics of the Population, 1870.*]

Chapter Seven

Educational Life and Institutions

Although the cause of education in America has always been considered of primary interest and importance, there does not . . . exist a regular and uniform system of instruction. The diversity of plans is almost as various as the several States of the Union are numerous. [E]ach State, in its sovereign capacity, has a right to devise and execute, and does execute, such provisions for the education of the people as are deemed expedient. Setting aside, therefore, a detailed account of all the existing plans, we can only consider in this place the characteristics of the school systems of the States in their collective capacity.

It should be remembered that the Federal Government is a most liberal patron of the schools in all parts of the country, and that a majority of the States have received large grants of land to be used for the support of educational institutions, and that they have appropriate officers to look after and expend the revenue derived from the sale of those lands. Ten years ago, the aggregated amount of money realized from the liberality of the General Government was about $50,000,000, but this amount has been annually increased since then. [W]hen to this fund we add the appropriations regularly made by the State Legislatures, we find that the total amount of money spent for educational purposes is truly enormous, and that in this particular . . . the States of America are unequalled by any other nation. Hence it is that there is ample provision made by the authorities alone, without including the munificent gifts of private individuals, to furnish every child in the land with a good education. And the black race, or Freemen, have the same privileges which are enjoyed by the whites.[1] Prior to the late rebellion, there existed no provision for the education of the colored race [in the slaveholding states]. But as soon

---

1. While the Freedman's Bureau did provide educational opportunities for newly freed African Americans, they certainly did not have the "same privileges" as whites in 1870.

as they became free measures were taken for their education, and in 1869 the total number who were known to be in attendance upon day, night, or Sunday schools, under the auspices of the Freedmen's Bureau, was upward of 250,000, and the freedmen paid out of their own earnings about $200,000 for tuition, and $125,000 for school-buildings.

COMMON SCHOOLS

[Let us] now proceed to submit a general account of the educational systems of the United States. We begin with the common-schools, the principle of which is the free elementary education of every child in the community, and which underlies the whole intellectual fabric of the American Republic. The system . . . originated in New England at the commencement of the present century [1800s] and was based upon the following ideas. First, the instruction of all the children in the State in the rudiments of an English education, viz.: reading, writing, elementary arithmetic and geography, and grammar. This to be accomplished by schools in every district. Second, each district to be independent of every other in all financial matters and management. Third, that there should be a superintendent or board of visitors in each town, generally consisting of professional men, and especially clergymen, to examine teachers, inspect the schools, and prescribe textbooks. Fourth, the support of these schools by taxation. Fifth, the power of compelling attendance on the part of the town authorities.

After an experience of nearly twenty years, it was found that the condition of the schools was not up to the demands of the time, and a revival in the cause of education took place, which resulted in greatly increasing the efficiency of the old system, until it was brought to a state of rare excellence, through the efforts of such men as Horace Mann [1796–1859] and Henry Barnard [1811–1900].[2] The school-system was again regenerated, and now possesses all the elements of the highest efficiency, the leading features of which are as follows. First, a system of graded schools for each town, embracing primary schools for the younger pupils; grammar-schools for the older, in which are taught, in addition to the common branches, philosophy, chemistry, history, drawing, music, algebra, geometry, and the French language. And high-schools for the more advanced, in which are taught the studies necessary for a business education, as well as the languages and the higher

---

2. Along with Horace Mann, Henry Barnard of Connecticut was a nationally renowned promoter of public education in the nineteenth century. Barnard became the first U.S. commissioner of education in 1867.

mathematics. Secondly, the employment of regular visitors, who are paid for their services. Thirdly, the enforcement of uniformity of textbooks, and regularity in attendance. Fourthly, regular and frequent public examination. Fifthly, the establishment of school libraries in connection with all the schools. Sixthly, the introduction of blackboards, globes, maps, charts, and other apparatus for instruction. Seventhly, the proper construction of schoolhouses. Eighthly, the establishment in every State of Normal schools for the instruction of regular teachers. Ninthly, the organization of State associations for comparison of methods of teaching, and the establishment of school periodicals. And, tenthly, the extension of the privileges of these schools to all the children of the school-age in each State, either by supporting the schools entirely by taxation and the income of funds where they exist, or by taxation and small rate bills, which are abated where they are unable to pay, and the furnishing of necessary books to the children of the poor.

That the above is a noble groundwork for the education of the masses must be acknowledged by all, and yet we find it a subject of serious complaint that the teachers in the common schools are not what they should be. In the great majority of cases, they are said to be too young and inexperienced, and that both the young men and young women employed look upon the office merely as a stepping-stone to better positions or more agreeable employments and not as a permanent business. An office under the Government, or a profession, will allure the young man from the schoolroom; and so also will an offer of marriage to the young woman. Of course there are many teachers whose knowledge, discipline, and nobleness of character, eminently fit them for their responsible posts, but they are not sufficiently numerous to form a class. It was this fact which caused a prominent writer on the subject to suggest that all badly-managed schools should be closed, and that the [closed school houses] should bear this inscription: "Poor teachers worse than no teachers."

. . . But notwithstanding this drawback, the common-schools of the country are a great national blessing. They are free and open to the poorest children in the community; but because these advantages are not always accepted by the people, in some of the States of the Union laws have been passed compelling a certain attendance at school. The [school] houses are comfortable, and conveniently located in every district where they are needed. The teachers are generally intelligent and circumspect in their lives and morals, and where they make teaching a regular profession, are all that could be reasonably expected or desired. With regard to their compensation there is no uniformity, but it is estimated to range from $39 to $57 per month for male teachers, with board; and from $27 to $30 per month for female teachers, with board. . . .

Nor is there . . . any uniformity in the management of the schools by the State authorities, and so, with a view of attempting to give a general idea of their condition we submit the following figures in regard to four of the representative States of the Republic. The number of students who attend school in the small State of Connecticut is 124,000; the amount expended in 1870 for school purposes was $11,269,152; and its school-fund was $2,046,108. In New York there are 1,000,000 children in the common-schools and 120,000 in the private schools; the school-houses are valued at $20,500,000; the amount paid to teachers, is $6,500,000; the amount expended in 1870 for instruction, nearly $10,000,000, and the school-fund is $11,300,000. In Pennsylvania, the students number 900,753; there are 14,212 schools; there are 17,612 teachers; school property is valued at $14,045,632; and annual expenses about $7,000,000. In Ohio, there are 740,382 students, and the school expenditures in 1870 amounted to $7,771,761. The total amount of school-fund in all the States is estimated at $50,000,000.

We give no figures in regard to any of the Southern States because the system of common-schools has never flourished in that region of the country, and because the late war has so deranged all public matters in those States that no statements at this time would do them full justice. Notwithstanding all that has been done in the United States for the cause of education, it has been estimated that the illiterate people of the country number about 6,000,000.[3]

With regard to the much discussed subject of the Bible in common-schools, we may submit the following remarks by a distinguished professor of Harvard University:

To banish the Bible was to garble history, for there was much history of which it was the only source. Christianity is the great factor in the history of the world. If more philosophy is to be taught, it must be Christian ethics. For the culture of the taste and imagination, the Bible transcends all other literature. Our English Bible has rendered important service in preserving our language. It is the key to the best English diction, and has helped to form the diction of every child. Our children should not be kept in ignorance of the fact that we are a Christian people. Sectarian religion should be excluded; but this can be done only by giving an unsectarian book, and the Bible is such a book. The Roman Catholics, in opposing the introduction of the Bible in common-schools, do not so much object to the book itself, but rather desire that the school-funds should be separated, which course the Protestants think would be detrimental to the welfare of the whole system.

---

3. The total population of the United States in 1870 was 39,818,449.

TEACHING SCHOOLS

With a view to enhancing the efficiency of the common-schools in the United States, there have been organized within the last few years a large number of Normal schools, the sole object of which is to educate a class of persons solely for the business of teaching, whereby very great good has already been accomplished in elevating the tone of instruction. At the present time there are fifty of these schools in successful operation in the Northern States, which are supported by the City or State Governments, and not less than thirty in the Southern States, for the benefit of the freedmen. The number of teachers already educated by them, including males and females, is estimated at two hundred thousand, and the pupils now being instructed about nine thousand. While there is no special uniformity in the management of these schools, we may obtain a general idea of their character by glancing at the features of a single one of them which has been particularly successful, the Normal University of Illinois. Candidates for admission to this institution . . . must have attained the age of sixteen; must produce certificates of good moral character; must sign a declaration that they intend to devote themselves to school-teaching in Illinois; and must pass a satisfactory examination in reading, spelling, writing, arithmetic, geography, and the elements of English grammar. The necessary annual expenses for each pupil range from ninety-seven to one hundred and eighty-eight dollars. There are five professors, and the term of study is usually three years. The course of instruction embraces the following subjects: metaphysics, methods of education, constitutions of the State and the United States, school-laws, English language, arithmetic, algebra, geometry, natural philosophy, book-keeping, geography, history, astronomy, chemistry, botany, physiology, geology, vocal music, and writing and drawing. The total number of pupils is three hundred; and there is an appendage to the institution called a model school, which contains five hundred pupils whose tuition is free, although they have to support themselves. While the Americans confess that their common-schools are not equal in efficiency to those of some other countries, they claim that this state of things cannot continue, and that their Normal schools . . . are unsurpassed.

HIGH SCHOOLS

Before an American youth can pass from a common-school into a college, he is obliged to go through a course of studies in what is called a high-school, or academy. These institutions are exceedingly varied in character, quite numerous, independent in organization, and very frequently originate in the liberality of private individuals. Although the instruction afforded by them is not gratuitous, the expenses are generally moderate. In some of them, however, provision is made by public appropriations for the education of such pupils [who] are too poor to pay. It often happens, however, that when young men are about to leave the academy or high-school, they conclude that their education has been sufficiently advanced for all practical purposes and so relinquish the idea of passing through college.

SCIENTIFIC, INDUSTRIAL, COMMERCIAL, MEDICAL, AND LAW SCHOOLS

And here, before describing the colleges and universities of America, we may with propriety allude to the present condition of the miscellaneous schools of the country. . . . The Sheffield Scientific School, which forms a part of Yale College, and the Lawrence Scientific School, connected with Harvard University, are both flourishing institutions, and are doing much to meet the wants of the age. Meanwhile there are [scientific] departments, standing on nearly the same basis, belonging to Brown University, Rutgers College, and the University of Michigan. As to Industrial Schools, there is also a great dearth of these in the United States. This is especially true in regard to Engineering and Navigation; and about all that is accomplished in the country in the way of anti-insruction, is accomplished by the National Academy and Cooper Institute of New York, the Athnaeum in Boston, the Academy of Arts in Philadelphia, and the Peabody Institute in Baltimore. In Massachusetts, New York, and Pennsylvania, they have Institutions of Technology. In California, there is a College of Mining and the Mechanic Arts, and associated with Agriculture. Attached to Columbia College, in New York, is a School of Mines. As to the advantages afforded by agricultural colleges, they are quite numerous. Well-endowed [agricultural] institutions are to be found in the States of Delaware, Illinois, Indiana, Iowa, Kansas, Kentucky, Maine, Maryland, Massachusetts (where there are several Japanese students), Michigan, Minnesota, New Hampshire, Pennsylvania, Vermont, West Virginia, and Wis-

---

4. At the time Mori wrote this, there were more Japanese students at Rutgers College in New Brunswick, New Jersey, than any other institution of higher learning in the United States. For studies of these earliest Japanese students in the United States, see Minoru Ishizuki, *Kindai Nihon no Kaigai Ryugakusei* (Rev. ed., Tokyo: Chuo Koronsha, 1992); James T. Conte, "Overseas Study in the Meiji Period: Japanese Students in America, 1867–1902" (Ph.D. diss., Princeton University, 1977); and chapter two, "*Ryugakusei*, Rutgers, and the American Experience" in John E. Van Sant, *Pacific Pioneers: Japanese Journeys to America and Hawaii, 1850–80* (Urbana and Chicago: University of Illinois Press, 2000).

consin.[4]

In none of the public schools of America are the foundation principles of commerce taught, and hence there have been established by private individuals what is called a "Chain of Commercial Colleges." These number not less than forty, and extend from Maine to Louisiana. Their course of instruction is very complete, and covers all that is necessary for a commercial life. And because this association is under one head, the regulations are such that a student, after completing a course of studies in one, may again take them up and pursue them at another school of the Chain without additional expense.

. . . The only school remaining to be mentioned under this miscellaneous head are those devoted to the study of medicine and law. The Medical Colleges and Schools of the country number fifty-one, and . . . as a competent writer has said, there have stood at the head of them men of learning, genius, and eminent distinction. And so there have also been, in the ranks of the profession, many physicians and surgeons of great ability and skill. But hardly any one who is acquainted with the status of medical education in America, will claim that either the distinguished professor, author, or practitioner, has owed his success in any considerable degree to the training of the school. As compared with the European standard, the training in America has been unsatisfactory to the last degree.

The Law Schools of the United States number twenty-two. It is said that, in at least one respect, they are superior to those of England [because] what they assume to do at all, they do more thoroughly and well. But it is no less true that they undertake very little in comparison with what is both attempted and accomplished in several of the European countries. In the form of departments, there are schools of law connected with many of the leading colleges; and in all of them the term of study is two years, the course of instruction being so arranged that a complete view is given during each year of the subjects embraced within it. The [law] professors number from one to five in each of these schools; a majority of them, in many instances, being judges of the Supreme Courts and resident lawyers in regular practice, whose services are gratuitous or partially compensated. The terms of admission are simply good morals and the age of eighteen years, and the fees, payable in advance, amount to one hundred dollars. The lawyers of the United States, as heretofore mentioned, have much to do with the making of the national laws, and the affairs of the General Government. A competent American critic has said, how few of them have been students of political economy, of civil polity, and of universal history. This is painfully manifest from the legislative discussions they hold and the laws they enact.

COLLEGES AND UNIVERSITIES

We come now to speak, in general terms, of the Collegiate Institutions of the United States. They are known as universities, colleges, seminaries, and institutes, and number in the aggregate not less than two hundred and eighty-five—exclusive of eighty-two in which theology is alone studied. While their courses of instruction embrace all branches of learning, it is almost invariably the case that something like a sectarian element pervades each institution, the only exceptions to this rule being those which are supported by the State governments. The number of institutions in America bearing the title of university is larger than in any other country, and a less number of them is said to have really any sort of claim to the title. On the other hand, there are several colleges which, though bearing that more modest name, are really entitled to be called universities. And then again there are seminaries and institutes which would seem, from their extent and high character, to be worthy of being called colleges. The precise meaning of the term university is a universal school, in which are taught all branches of learning, or the four faculties of theology, medicine, law, and the sciences and arts. A college is a school incorporated for purposes of instruction, where the students may acquire a knowledge of the languages and sciences. The idea of a seminary or an academy is allied to that of a college, only that the former are more especially designed for a younger class of students. [A]n institute is a literary or philosophical society formed by persons for their mutual instruction and advantage in all matters connected with intellectual culture. The so-called universities of America number one hundred, while the other collegiate institutions are about equally divided between the three remaining classes. . . . The reader may obtain a general idea of their character by glancing at a few of the more influential and prominent institutions.

Harvard College, located at Cambridge, Massachusetts, and founded in 1636, is the oldest institution of learning in America. It has twenty-eight professors and about five hundred students. Although it has hitherto had a liberal divinity school, arrangements have recently been made for incorporating in it an "Episcopal Theological School." It has a Law department, with three professors; a Medical department, with eleven professors; a School of Astronomy, with two professors; a Dental School, with seven professors; a Museum of Zoology, with lectures by four professors; and the Lawrence Scientific School, and School of Mining and Practical Geology, with seven professors. Its general and special libraries comprise one hundred and fifty thousand volumes, and its scientific collections are extensive and of great value. It is managed by one president, five fellows, one treasurer, and thirty overseers chosen by the State Legislature. Its endowment fund, derived from numerous individuals and corporations, and independent of the college grounds, building, libraries, and collections, is somewhat over two millions of dollars; and its annual income is about one hundred and eighty thousand dollars. The term of study in the law school is two years; in the divinity school three; and candidates for the degree of doctor of medicine must have studies of three years, and attended two courses of lectures.

The next oldest institution of learning in America is Yale College, founded at New Haven, Connecticut, in 1700. It has about sixty professors, and usually seven hundred students. Besides an academic department, it has five others, devoted to philosophy, theology, law, medicine, and the fine arts. Its miscellaneous collections are extensive and very valuable, and its libraries comprise about eighty-five thousand volumes. The total amount of its funds available for the support of the college is something over one million of dollars. This college differs from Harvard chiefly in the constitution of its department of philosophy and the arts, which has come to be known as the Sheffield Scientific School. Candidates for admission are obliged to be sixteen years of age, and to undergo a twofold examination, first in mathematical studies, and secondly in elementary literary studies. The charge for tuition is one hundred and twenty-five dollars, but students of chemistry have to pay an additional sum of seventy-five dollars. The term of study in each of the courses is three years; and in the divinity school no charge is made for tuition.

Another college of note and influence is Columbia College, founded in the city of New York in 1754, but prior to 1787 it was known as King's College. Its funds, derived chiefly from donations, amount to two millions of dollars; its professors about fifty, and the usual number of students is nine hundred. It has four departments, devoted to Letters and Science, Mines, Law, and Medicine. The charges for tuition range from one hundred to one hundred and sixty dollars per annum. Several societies and municipal corporations are entitled to several scholarships free of charge. Every religious denomination in the city of New York is entitled always to have one student free of all charges for tuition. And every school from which there shall be admitted four matriculants in any year is also allowed to send one pupil free of charge.

The College of New Jersey, located at Princeton, is another of the venerable institutions of the United States. It was founded in 1746, has about twenty professors, and nearly three hundred students. It is supported by the Presbyterians, and has educated nearly nine hundred men for the ministry. Princeton charges a tuition fee of seventy dollars, and has a choice library of twenty-five thousand volumes.

In Georgetown, District of Columbia, there is a Roman Catholic College [Georgetown University], founded in 1792, with twenty professors, two hundred students, and a library of thirty thousand volumes. In Brunswick, Maine, is located Bowdoin College, founded in 1802, and possessing a library of thirty-seven thousand volumes. In New Hampshire they have Dartmouth College, founded in 1769, supported by the Congregationalists, and with thirty-eight thousand volumes in its library. In Pennsylvania, Dickinson College, founded in 1783, is supported by the Methodists and has twenty-five thousand volumes. In Rhode Island, Brown University, founded in 1764, is supported by the Baptists, and has a library of thirty-eight thousand volumes. And in Virginia, a State University, founded in 1819, has thirty-five thousand volumes. There are several institutions, which have more recently been founded, and which are growing with great rapidity and exercising a paramount influence in the educational world: the Universities of Michigan, Kentucky, and Illinois, and the Cornell University in New York.

Another institution which deserves special mention, because of its extent and peculiar character: Vassar College, is located at Poughkeepsie, New York. It was founded in 1861, through the liberality of one man, Matthew Vassar, and is wholly devoted to the education of women. The buildings are extensive and beautiful. The school offers the highest educational facilities to females at moderate expense, and admits as beneficiaries those who are unable to pay even that expense. Special attention is devoted to the fine arts, and it has a corps of instructors in the English language and literature, the modern languages of Europe and their literature, ancient languages, mathematics, all the branches of natural science, including anatomy, physiology, hygiene, intellectual and moral philosophy, political economy and the science of government, domestic economy, and the study of the Scriptures, without sectarianism.[5]

Notwithstanding the fact that the educational records of the United States are very complete, and the amount of money annually expended in the cause is very large, it would seem that the requirements of the age and of America have not as yet by any means been attained. An American writer, in an elaborate report on this subject, published at the national expense, has summed up his opinions in a single paragraph, as follows: To tell the plain truth, he says,

> the very best of our many universities are but sorry skeletons of the well-developed and shapely institutions they ought to be and must become, before they will be fairly entitled to rank among the foremost universities of even this present day. And if we are not content always to suffer the contempt of European scholars, who properly enough regard us as a very clever, but also a very un-

5. The first Japanese women to study at universities in the United States, Nagai Shigeko and Yamakawa Sutematsu, attended and graduated from Vassar College in the 1880s. See Akiko Kuno, *Unexpected Destinations: The Poignant Story of Japan's First Vassar Graduate* (Tokyo: Kodansha International, 1993).

cultured people, it is time that all true lovers of learning, as well as all who desire the highest prosperity and glory of America, should awake to the importance of at once providing the means of a profounder, broader, and higher culture in every department of human learning.

As the education of women is a subject which possesses a peculiar interest for the people of Japan, we here submit a few observations in that connection. In America, females possess precisely the same advantages for education that are possessed by the males. Boys and girls are admitted to the same schools, and the gentle influences of the latter are counterbalanced by the elevating influences of the former, whereby it is thought that both classes are improved. At the same time, there are thousands of schools in which the two sexes are instructed separately. The idea is universal that the women of the country are capable of receiving, and should receive, the highest kind of education. As to the question of their right to take part in politics by voting, which has been extensively discussed in America, it seems to be one of those problems which the future alone can establish. The important part which the women of America take in educational affairs is shown by the following facts. They are educated at the Normal schools for the express purpose of becoming teachers. They officiate as teachers in thousands of the common-schools. Seminaries for the education of young ladies are to be found in every part of the country. They are admitted into several of the American colleges as regular students, and that a number of institutions of the highest character are exclusively devoted to the education of women, the most extensive and interesting, Vassar College, having already been mentioned.[6] Not only are the libraries of the country regularly visited and used by ladies (in some of which they are employed as librarians), but in the leading cities are to be found libraries and reading-rooms designed for their use exclusively, and all of them in harmony with the idea of American civilization.

---

6. Nevertheless, the majority of colleges and universities in the United States, as in Europe, did not admit women as regular students until the early twentieth century.

Chapter Eight

Literary, Artistic, and Scientific Life

BOOKS, AUTHORS, AND PUBLISHING

Under the heading of literary life, we propose to submit some information on the book publishing and newspaper interests of the United States. When an author has written a book, whether large or small, and desires to profit by its publication, he is obliged to take out a copyright by which the Government promises to protect his rights for a term of years in the profits of the work as his own property. The document in question is used under the law by the Librarian of Congress, and two copies of every book or pamphlet published have to be deposited in the National Library, whereby the collection of volumes belonging to the Government is annually increased to a large extent. . . .

As to the subjects upon which books are written, they are, of course, very numerous. The general heads under which they are arranged being as follows: theology and religion, poetry, history, biography, geography and travels, philosophy, science, social reform, school-books, useful and fine arts, fiction, literature, miscellaneous books, republications and translations from foreign authors. With many men as well as women, the writing of books is a special business. And then again there are thousands of books written merely as a pastime by their authors, or from motives of personal vanity.

Generally speaking, the writers do not find the business profitable; but there are authors who make a great deal of money by writing—especially is this the case with school-books, novels, and national histories. The men who print and sell the books . . . are called publishers, and in all the principal cities are to be found establishments which do business on a very large scale. Some of them give employment to large numbers of people, such as writers, paper-makers, printers, binders, artists of various kinds, and machinists, as well as clerks and common workmen, and not a few have acquired very large fortunes by this branch of industry. They usually sell books by the quantity alone, and the retail merchants who purchase them are to be found in every town and village in the whole land. When an author has written a book, he either sells his copyright to the publisher for a specific sum of money, after which he has nothing to do with his work; or else he allows the publisher the privilege of printing and selling his book, charging for the same a certain per centum on the price of each volume, [while] retaining the ownership of the work in his own name. While many of the books published are so interesting or valuable as to be purchased by everybody interested in the subject, very many of them can only be sold by means of extravagant notices in the newspapers and hence the custom prevails of sending most of all the new books to the newspapers, which pretend to give impartial notices but often do the very reverse.

The custom of reading books among the people of America is almost universal, far more so, it is said, than is the case in England or France. In every home, from that of the rich merchant down to the poorest farmer, may generally be found such collections of books as they desire or can afford to buy. And for those who cannot afford to purchase all they may wish to read, in the cities and towns everywhere they have circulating libraries where, for a small consideration, books may be read, or borrowed, to be read at home. In most of the leading cities collections of this sort have been established which are very extensive and valuable. The good which these libraries accomplish, by furnishing the people with information on every conceivable subject, cannot be estimated . . . and the largest in the country, which is called the National Library and located in Washington City, contains not less than 200,000 volumes and is entirely free to all who may desire to consult its treasures. In 1860, there were 27,730 libraries in the country, in which were collected nearly 14,000,000 volumes.

THE POWER OF THE PRESS

The most striking feature connected with the literature of America is the universal circulation of newspapers and magazines, which are read by all classes of the people. . . . According to the latest accounts, the whole number of periodicals issued in the United States and its Territories is 6,056. Of these 637 are published daily, 118 tri-weekly, 129 semi-weekly, 4,612 weekly, 21 bi-weekly, 100 semi-monthly, 715 monthly, 14 bi-monthly, and 62 are issued quarterly. Of this large number it is estimated that about four-fifths are political journals, the remainder being religious or literary. It is through these numerous publications that the mind of the nation is chiefly expressed, and its intellectual pulse may generally be measured by the success of the several journals. While very many of these have a circulation which is confined to their particular religious sect or political party, there are a few whose circulation is immense, and their influence proportionably extensive. For example, there is one weekly paper published in New York which has a circulation of 175,000, and if we estimate that each paper is read by five persons, which is not unlikely, we perceive that each issue has the teaching of 875,000 minds. And then again, there are some daily papers which issue every morning from 100,000 to 200,000 copies. As far back as 1860, it was estimated that the circulation of the newspapers alone amounted to 100,000,000. Hence we perceive that the power of the Press is enormous, and it is a matter of the utmost importance that it should be conducted with honesty and wisdom. That portion of it which comes under the head of newspapers is by far the most profitable, so far as making money is concerned, but the profit does not come from selling the paper alone. In all of them certain columns or pages are filled up with advertisements, and as these are paid for on liberal terms, they become a source of profit. . . .

With these figures before us, we cannot wonder that what is called the Press of America should be considered an element of almost incalculable power. As has well been said, it records with fidelity the proceedings of Congress, of all State and Territorial legislatures, and of judicial tribunals, holds the pulpit to a just responsibility, reviews the doings of business and social life, and watches with sleepless vigilance over the concerns of the people. It is the great representative of the people; a conservative power held by them to guard both public and industrial liberty; reflecting their opinions and judgments in all matters respecting the public weal; exposing wrong, and vindicating and encouraging the right.

In writing for the newspapers of America, many of the ablest men are employed, and the leading writer for each journal is called an editor. He is frequently the sole proprietor, sometimes only owns a few shares in the enterprise, and then again he may be hired to perform a specific editorial duty. He is responsible for the opinions expressed, and when necessary, as is always the case in the larger establishments, he is assisted in his labors by sub-editors who look after all matters connected with commerce or literature. [The editor is also assisted] by reporters who prepare the proceedings of public assemblies; and by correspondents who furnish information on every subject of public interest. Weekly papers are commonly published on Saturday of each week, and daily papers in the morning or evening. As most of the latest news is received through the telegraph, it is frequently the case that an evening paper will publish information of an event which may have taken place in Europe on the morning of the same day. With regard to what is called the liberty of the press, in times of peace it is quite unbounded. So much so, indeed, that the rights of private citizens are not always respected. While an editor may not be interfered with by the government for expressing his opinions, provided they are not immoral, it is too often the case that his real independence is materially affected by the allurements or dictation of the political party to which he belongs. And then again, the habit of dealing in personalities is perhaps more prevalent among the newspaper writers of America than among any other people; the excesses in this direction sometimes lead to bitter conflicts and even to untimely deaths. It is certain that all the more notorious abuses of the Press are frowned upon by the better classes in every community. Notwithstanding its many drawbacks, the conclusion is inevitable that the Press of America is the leading civilizer of its multifarious population, and the particular engine which has brought about the present prosperous condition of the Republic.

PAINTING, SCULPTURE, AND ARCHITECTURE

Our next topic for consideration is the artistic life of America as we find it developed in the pursuits of painting, sculpture, and architecture. The number of persons engaged in these various employments is not large, but they are necessarily men of culture. [These artists] exert a great influence in developing the taste of the people generally, and they congregate and find employment chiefly in the larger cities.

The painters are of several kinds: portrait painters, historical painters, landscape painters, and various subordinate classes who produce miscellaneous pictures. The materials most commonly used are oil-colors and canvas. While the majority of these artists manage to support themselves in comfort, those who happen to become fashionable or possess extraordinary ability frequently meet with great success. It is true that good portraits may be obtained for fifty or one hundred dollars; it is also true that five thousand dollars is not an uncommon price for very superior portraits. According to circumstances, the prices paid for pictures of scenery range from fifty dollars to ten thousand dollars. In these two departments, the American artists are perhaps equal to those of Europe. But with regard to historical painting, the English, French, and German artists are all in advance of the Americans. Generally speaking, before a man can become expert in the art of painting, he has to acquire a knowledge of drawing, and this study has come to be so common and popular that many artists confine themselves to drawing alone, and hence the kind of pictures known as engravings, which are merely copies of drawings, as well as painting, have almost a universal circulation. They are executed on steel, on copper, on stone, and on wood, and used extensively in books and weekly and monthly periodicals. To what extent this is true, is shown by the fact that a single illustrated journal, published in New York, is said to have a circulation of three hundred thousand copies.[1] And then again, large numbers of engravings are prepared and published, which are used for the adornment of the houses of the people, as is the case with paintings, as well as photographs, and chromolithographs, which latter classes of pictures have come to be more popular than any others. The custom of hanging pictures on the walls of the houses is a leading characteristic among the Americans. While the poor mechanic or farmer may be content with a few cheap engravings or photographs, men of wealth are very much in the habit of spending thousands upon thousands of dollars for works of art of the highest order. Many of the private collections thus formed are really of a princely character. In all the leading cities they have extensive public collections of pictures, with which are commonly associated certain schools for imparting a practical knowledge of the fine arts. The extent to which the General Government patronizes the art of painting is limited to a few historical productions, including compositions and portraits, to be found in the Capitol and Executive Mansion [of the White House].

As the art of sculpture is far less popular among the people than that of painting, we find the sculptors reduced to a small number. Among them, however, are to be found some few men of great abilities and extensive reputations. It is claimed, indeed, that the United States has gained in sculpture a far higher rank than in any of the fine arts. The works here produced are generally executed in white marble, though sometimes in bronze, and in the great majority of instances represent the busts or full-length figures of distinguished men. This style of art is always expensive, and it is only the rich who can afford to perpetuate the features of their family-friends in this manner. When intended for exhibition in private dwellings, or in galleries of art, these productions are usually of the size of life, but when intended for the adornment of private gardens or public grounds they are of colossal size, and noted military men are occasionally represented mounted on horses. The chief patrons of this kind of art are the National and State Governments, and hence busts and statues are to be found . . . in the public buildings in Washington and in the capitals of the several States. In the National Capitol a large and handsome hall has been appropriated entirely to the reception of busts and statues of celebrated statesmen, and military and naval commanders. In this connection, a law has been passed granting the privilege to each State in the

---

1. Probably a reference to *Harper's Weekly*.

Union to send to this central exhibition-place a portrait, in marble, of any two men which the State authorities may choose to honor in this manner. When copies of marble or bronze productions are desired by private individuals, and the means of the person wanting them are limited, it is frequently the case that a kind of white plaster is used as a substitute for the more enduring materials. This composition is employed, to a great extent, in reproducing the ancient and more celebrated works of sculpture in Europe, which are brought to America to serve as models in the art schools of the country.

We come now to speak of what has been done in the United States in the way of architecture. In the early years of the country the abundance of wood, and the ease of preparing it, made it the universal building material, and for a long time hardly anything else was used; although for buildings of importance brick was brought from England. The haste to get shelter, and the availability of wood, make this still the common material—almost the only one used—in the new cities of the Western States and Territories. The recent [October 8–9, 1871] terrible fire at Chicago is an illustration, in part, of this fact, and of the evils of building with wood alone. But within the present century much brick has been made, and stone-quarries have been opened all over the country. In the older cities, brick and stone, in connection with iron, are now almost entirely employed . . . . The New England States furnish a great deal of granite and sienite, which are very strong and durable stones, but too hard and rough for finely cut or ornamental work. There is much sandstone in the Middle States, and in the West are many kinds of sand and limestone, which are easily cut, and receive readily the richest ornamentation. There is also throughout the United States a great variety of white and colored marbles, much used in ornamental and decorative work, and many elaborate buildings are built of them.

Before the present century architects were few in America and of little skill, and buildings were designed, for the most part, by the men who built them. But the gain of the community in wealth and leisure has greatly developed the profession in the present generation. The earlier architects worked only by English traditions, which were, in their turn, derived from the Italian architects of the sixteenth and seventeenth centuries. The earlier architects of this country usually obtained their professional education in Europe, where the advantages were numerous. At the present time, however, young Americans find excellent opportunities in the offices of the better-trained architects at home. The multiplication of prints, photographs, and casts in plaster from the best old examples, have greatly facilitated study. Schools of architecture have been established in several of the educational institutions of the country, and in New York they have an American Institute of Architects, which is represented in all the leading cities of the country by what they call "Chapters."

The styles of architecture employed in America are as various as possible, but perhaps the kind of buildings in which the United States architects are most successful is that of wooden villas, which are often both beautiful and convenient. It has been charged against the Americans that in regard to architecture, if nothing else, they lay more stress upon the idea of a conventional beauty, than upon substantial usefulness. A church may be beautiful to the eye, but filled with uncomfortable seats and a perpetual darkness; a public building may be very ornamental, but badly ventilated; and a dwelling may appear like a palace, and in reality be without a single comfort. Notwithstanding the immense amounts of money which are annually expended in America upon fine buildings, it is claimed that there is much room for improvement. It is a creditable truth that a great impetus has recently been given to the art of architecture by the patronage of the General Government whose buildings are numerous, and among the most extensive and imposing in the Republic. In this connection, one fact which seems amazing . . . is this: that there now stands in the city of Washington a monument to the memory of George Washington, who is called the Father of his Country, which was commenced a quarter of a century ago, and is yet unfinished and a painful spectacle to all the world.

SCIENCE

We come now to speak of science in America, but before doing so it may be proper to make some remarks in regard to science in general. The term science, in its more restricted sense, is a knowledge of the laws of nature, or how the changes in the natural world are produced. In a more general sense it is used to include descriptive natural history, from which it . . . classifies and describes things or objects in nature as they exist, without considering their origin or the changes to which they are subjected. Science, then, although founded on the results of experiments and observations, does not consist in collections of isolated facts, but in general principles from which special facts can be deduced when certain conditions are known. Thus, the phenomena of astronomy are all referred to principles which are denominated the laws of force and motion. By means of these laws, if the relative mass, position, and velocity of the heavenly bodies are known at a given epoch, their relative position for all times, in the remotest past as well as in the distant future can be calculated. Other phenomena are referred to other laws, such as those of light, heat, electricity, navigation, chemical action, life, and organization. These laws are generally expressed in the form of theories, by which they can be more readily understood and applied, either in the way of practical inventions, or in the discovery of new truths. The knowledge of a law of nature enables the savant to explain, predict, and in some cases to control the phenomena to which these laws pertain. These characteristics of science afford the means of clearly distinguishing between the expressions of real truths or laws, and the mere vague speculations with which the principles of science are often confounded.

It is by the discovery and application of these laws that modern civilization differs essentially from that of ancient times, and also from the civilizations of China and Japan. In these countries the arts of life are based upon facts accidentally discovered, which lie on the face of nature, are few in number, and soon exhausted. While in Europe and North America the various inventions which add so much to the material well-being of man are derived from the endless stores of facts deduced from scientific principles. It is by a knowledge of the law of gravitation, heat, electricity, and chemical action, that these powers are rendered obedient and efficient slaves, by which man emancipates himself from the bondage of brute labors, to which in ancient times he was universally subjected. While by a knowledge of the laws of light and of sound, the infirmities of age are remedied and the range of human senses indefinitely extended. By the constant study of the phenomena of nature, irrespective of the use which may flow from them, our knowledge is continually increased while from the discovery of every new principle in science many applications in art usually follow. It is this which is understood by the Baconian aphorism, "Knowledge is power." There are at the present time, in all parts of the civilized world, men who are devoting their thoughts and time to the investigations of the various phenomena of nature, and through the intercourse which is established between all parts of the world, the discoveries made by each become the knowledge of all, and in this way science is rapidly increasing. Moreover, whatever is discovered in one portion of the domain of nature, as a general rule, tends to reflect light on various other portions and also to furnish instruments for more extended and varied research.

It is evident . . . that the country is most highly civilized . . . which makes the best provision for the investigation of abstract science. Of all nations at present existing, Prussia appears to be the most advanced in this respect. Whenever an individual is found capable of making original discoveries in that country, he is at once consecrated to science. He is elected a higher professor in one of the universities, receives a liberal salary, is supplied with all the implements necessary for research in his special line, and is allowed full time for his investigations being required to give but few lectures on higher subjects while the teaching and the drilling of pupils are performed by men of inferior talents. In the United States, where so much is to be done in the way of subduing nature and developing the resources of a new country, there has been, consequently, a great demand for the application of science and less attention has been given until of late, to encourage and sustain original invention.

One effect of the general diffusion of education in the United States, especially in New England, has been to render the people impatient as to mere manual labor and hence, from the scarcity of laborers and the great demand for them, a large amount of talent has been devoted to the invention of labor-saving machines. There are no people in the world who make so many inventions as the Americans, which fact is evinced by the number and variety of models in the Patent Office. There is, however, a growing inclination on the part of the Government and of wealthy individuals to endow establishments for the advance of pure science. The Government has established the National Observatory, which is supported at an annual expense of not less than seventy-five thousand dollars, and in which the motions of the heavenly bodies are continuously studied, new facts observed, and new deductions from them constantly made. There has also been established a Bureau for the calculation of a Nautical Almanac, the object of which is to furnish mariners with the means for determining their position on the ocean, while it also contributes to the advance of science by original mathematical deductions from facts which have been observed. An extended work called the Coast Survey has likewise been established, the object of which is to furnish accurate maps by means of astronomical determinations, of the whole coast of the country, but which also is developing in its operations new facts of the highest interest to science. Among those are the laws of the variation, direction, and intensity of terrestrial magnetism—the form and dimensions of the earth—the variation of the force of terrestrial gravitation on the different portions of the earth's surface—the knowledge of organized beings which live at the bottom of the ocean, within soundings—and temperature, motion, and magnitude of the Gulf Stream, which, in passing across the Atlantic Ocean, moderates the temperature and gives a genial climate to the north of Europe. Another of the Government establishments which advances science is the office of Weights and Measures, in which a series of investigations are carried on for determining the expansion of bodies and the best manner of making accurate standards of measure, of length, weight, and capacity. The Government also has its schools of applied science; one at West Point for the education of officers of the army in all things pertaining to military life and operations; and another at Annapolis, for the education of naval officers in all matters connected with the naval service. Of late years, moreover, numerous surveys and explorations have been made at the expense of the Government, across the Continent, which have tended, not only to develop the resources of the country but have afforded means for the critical study of the geology, mineralogy, and natural history of the regions traversed, and which have resulted in the construction of the celebrated rail-road between the Atlantic and Pacific Oceans. In many of the older States of the Union there have been instituted geological surveys which, while they have served to discover the peculiar mineral treasures within the State limits, have greatly added to the science of geology as well as to natural history. The ostensible object of all these establishments of the General Government, as well as those of the separate States, is practical utility, although abstract science is greatly advanced by means of them.

In various parts of the country astronomical observatories have been erected in connection with some of the principal universities and colleges, but in them, with but few exceptions, original investigations are subordinate to the business of education. There are also connected with the higher institutions of learning, scientific schools, the object of which is generally to teach the principles of science, as far as they are applicable to civil and mining engineering, and the various manufactures which depend upon a knowledge of chemistry and physics. The professors in universities and colleges are the principal contributors to the scientific journals of the day, in which the progress of science is recorded. There is no civilized country in which there appears to be a greater taste for a knowledge of general scientific results, or in which a greater number of popular scientific works are read than in the United States. At the same time, there is scarcely any country in which original talents, applied to pure scientific investigation, meet with less reward. In France and other European countries there are Academies of Science, consisting of a limited number of the most distinguished individuals, and supported by Government, each member receiving a salary, besides marks of social distinction. To become a member of one of these academies is an object of the highest ambition, to which is directed the best minds of the community. In Great Britain there are no such academies, yet the Government makes yearly grants for scientific investigations; and individuals, distinguished for their scientific discoveries, not only receive pensions, but are honored by the titles of barons and knights. No adequate inducements are yet held out in the United States as a stimulus to scientific investigation, but for scientific invention or the application of science to useful arts, there is frequently an abundant remuneration. Notwithstanding these drawbacks, much has been done . . . in the way of advancing science, as is evinced by the transactions of the American Philosophical Society of Philadelphia, of the American Academy of Arts and Sciences of Boston, the publications of the Smithsonian Institution, and of the Natural History Societies and Academies of Boston, Salem, Philadelphia, Chicago, San Francisco, and New Orleans. All these institutions were established and are sustained by private individuals. . . .

A large portion of the scientific labor of the United States has been devoted to descriptive natural history, to which attention was invited by the almost unbounded field which was presented for study in the mineral, vegetable, and animal kingdoms, and because a knowledge derived from these was intimately connected with the development of the wealth and prosperity of the country. Science should, however, be studied for its own sake, without regard to its immediate application, since nothing tends more to extend the bounds of thought, to add to the intellectual powers of man, and to raise him in the scale of intelligence, than the study and contemplation of the operations of nature. And we are happy to think that, as we have said before, there is in this great country a growing appreciation of the importance of abstract science, and that many institutions in various parts of it will be established, through the enlightened policy of wealthy individuals, for its cultivation and advancement. A conspicuous example of what has been done in this line is the Smithsonian Institution, founded in Washington by James Smithson of England, for the increase and diffusion of knowledge among men. The founder was devoted to scientific investigation, and under the impulse of his ruling passion bequeathed his entire property for a similar purpose. It is as yet the only well-endowed institution in America which is intended exclusively for the advancement of abstract science. But through the influence which it has attained by the persevering effort of its director, Prof. Joseph Henry [1797–1878], and the example which it has set, it is thought that other institutions of a similar character will be founded. . . .[2]

---

2. Joseph Henry, prominent scientist, inventor, and the first Director of the Smithsonian Institution. Despite the nearly half-century difference in their ages, Henry and Mori became good friends during Mori's years as Japan's chargé d'affaires in Washington, D.C.

Chapter Nine

Life among the Miners

It is now generally acknowledged that the mineral resources of the United States are more extensive and varied than those of any other country in the world. Indeed, to give anything like a minute account of them would fill many volumes. Therefore, with a view of being brief, we propose to submit a few facts on the leading mineral productions of the country, beginning with the precious metals.

GOLD AND SILVER

Gold has been found in about one-half of the States of the Union. Prior to the year 1848 this metal, as well as silver, was chiefly obtained from Virginia, Tennessee, the Carolinas, and Georgia. At the present time the States of California, Oregon, and Nevada, and the Territories of Washington, Idaho, Arizona, Colorado, New Mexico, Montana, Dakota, and Wyoming are by far the most productive gold-fields on the globe. Throughout all this region many other valuable minerals are found, but silver is the most important. At the time of the great discoveries in California [1848–1849], the annual production of the whole world was only $20,000,000; but in seven years from that time California alone yielded $60,000,000, and its recent annual production has been fixed at $80,000,000. The total gold and silver product of the United States down to the year 1868 was estimated at $1,255,000,000, and never before in the history of the world have so few people established so extensive a business. The region where gold is found covers an area of 1,000,000 square miles and is chiefly the property of the nation. Hand-washing, as we have been informed by a man of experience in these matters, was the earliest mode of collecting gold, and the pan and the rocker were the first implements used in California mining. Quicksilver was soon employed to collect the fine particles often lost in hand-washing. Hydraulic mining, now largely used in California, is done by throwing currents of water from hose and pipes with enormous force against banks of earth, cutting away whole hills. Down the face of the hills pour artificial streams. At the foot, the waters all pass away in long flumes or wooden troughs, carrying the earth and stones with them. Slats on the bottom of the flumes catch and retain the gold. And where gold is found in hard quartz, the stones are ground to powder by machinery and stamp-mills, and the gold thus comes to the light, and quicksilver separates it from the dust.

Silver is never found like gold, in grains among the sand, but in ores or quartz from which it has to be reduced by stamping or grinding or by smelting. It is found in a variety of ores, usually associated with gold, copper, or lead. Pure masses are occasionally found among the copper mines of Lake Superior, and also in Nevada and Idaho. The discovery of the rich deposits of gold and silver in California gave new impetus to the movements of populations everywhere, stimulated all departments of industry, brought together into the same communities people from every part of the globe, settled the vast territories of the United States, facilitated intercourse between the nations, and, with the mining operations in Australia, has steadily changed values throughout the world.

Notwithstanding the immense amount of treasure that has been taken from the soils and rocks of California and other Pacific States, the business of mining has not been profitable with the majority of miners. Indeed, it is said that during the last fifteen years, the farmers of Illinois have more frequently made fortunes than have the gold-hunters of the West. In 1865 a miner of California named Jules Fricot realized the sum of $182,511 by quartz mining, and since then a man named James P. Pierce, from placer mine obtained in one year the sum of $102,011. But these were exceptional cases. The cost of living at the mines is always expensive, and the accommodations anything but comfortable. At the general eating-houses which are established among the mines, they commonly charge one dollar for a single meal, and twelve dollars per week for board, with the sleeping accommodations being a bare floor and a pair of blankets. According to the latest authentic data, the number of miners in California alone was 46,660, of whom 20,800 were Chinese, and the wages of these men ranged from three to five dollars per day. The national laws bearing upon the mining region of the Pacific Slope are not, as yet, what they should be. Those laws which have been enacted provide for two classes of miners—those who are licensed to work upon the public domain, and those who become actual proprietors by purchase from the Government. The right is also granted to men to purchase and work such mines as they may discover. . . .

And now, in closing these remarks, let us glance at what has been said in regard to the distribution of the precious metals. The drain of them has hitherto been toward the East [i.e., Asia], where they are used for hoarding and for ornaments, rather than for money. This is particularly true of silver. Between the years 1850 and 1864, there were exported to Asia from England and the Mediterranean more than $650,000,000. The total amount of silver in the world is estimated at $10,000,000,000, or only enough to pay the debts of three or four of the leading nations of the present time. The coining of gold and silver, as well as copper, was commenced by the United States in 1793, and the total product of each metal, down to the middle of 1870, was as follows: Gold, $971,628,046; silver, $143,760,474; copper, $11,009,048; or a grand total of $1,126,397,569.

COPPER AND COAL

Of the baser metals which have hitherto been employed in the coining of money, copper is the most important. Its most valuable alloy is brass, out of which a very large number of useful things are manufactured. Another alloy, known as "French gold," is extensively used in the manufacture of cheap jewelry and watches. Copper is found in ores and in a metallic state, and was first mined on the American Continent in New England. It has been worked in seven or eight of the States but practically all the copper product of the Union comes from Lake Superior, which was almost an unknown wilderness as late as the year 1843. It is found in a ridge of trap-rock, on the shores belonging to Michigan, and masses of the solid metal have been discovered weighing several tons. The mines were opened there in 1845, since which time then total yield has been not far from 150,000 tons. It is extracted from its ores by smelting and calcination, and prepared for the market in ingots, which are converted into sheets by rolling mills established chiefly in the Atlantic States. Situated as are the copper mines of Michigan, in a region where the winters are long and the summers short, the miners are subject to many hardships from the cold and to many privations in the way of bodily comforts. A large proportion of them are men who have had experience in the mines of Great Britain and other countries, and their compensation is not on a par with their habits of industry and their experience, but the quantity of metal which they obtain from the earth and send to market is very large.

Next in importance to the precious metals, come the coal productions of the United States, the two prominent varieties of which bear the names of anthracite and bituminous. The largest producer of both is the State of Pennsylvania. In the production of the former, Rhode Island stands second; [while]

Ohio occupies the second position in regard to bituminous coal. The area of workable coal-beds in the United States, excluding Alaska, is estimated at 200,000 square miles, which is said to be eight times as large as the available coal area of all the rest of the world. The coal-veins are usually reached by vertical shafts, but when found in hills are worked by horizontal galleries. Notwithstanding the fact that perpendicular shafts are employed to secure thorough ventilation, and safety-lamps are used to prevent the ignition of the fatal fire-damp, many serious accidents have happened in the mines of Pennsylvania. The first railway for the transmission of coal from the mines was built in 1827, and the coal mines now give employment to more than forty railroads and canals. It is a common occurrence for a train of 100 cars to enter the city of Philadelphia, loaded with anthracite, and the same may be said of Baltimore, which is the principal exporting place for bituminous coal. The total product of the United States for the year 1868 was about 19,000,000 tons, valued at $26,000,000, since which time these figures have been increased, and are still increasing. It is now seventy years since anthracite coal was used as fuel in this country, and about forty years since it began to be extensively mined in the United States. It has been stated by authentic writers on the subject, that the coal-fields of the United States are thirty-six times greater than those of Great Britain, while the annual production of Britain is five times greater than that of the United States. The reasons for this great difference are apparent. In many of the States of the Union, the climate is so mild that no coal is needed for domestic purposes, and when fuel is demanded for manufacturing purposes, there is always to be obtained an abundant supply of wood. And then again, excepting the New England, the Middle, and some of the Western States where prairies abound, the forests are so numerous that it must be many years before coal will become a necessity among the people. Indeed, the very remarkable fact has been chronicled, that in some of the Western States, where agriculture is the chief source of wealth, the article known as maize, or Indian corn, has been employed as fuel.

PETROLEUM

If, however, we find that a large proportion of the inhabitants in America have no immediate interest in the production of coal, it is at the same time true, that a very large part of the population are consumers of what is called coal-oil, or petroleum. Although long known to the scientific world, this article did not become known to the commercial world until 1858. It is found in various parts of the country, but more extensively in western Pennsylvania than in any other region, where very large fortunes have been made by persons engaged in drawing the precious liquid out of the earth. It is obtained by means of artesian wells, which are sunk from one hundred to six hundred feet into the earth, and some of which have yielded, with the aid of forcing-pumps, as much as two thousand barrels of oil in a single day. The applications of petroleum are chiefly limited to purposes of illumination and lubricating machinery, and for the latter purpose the consumption is very large on the railroads and in the manufactories. A distillation of this oil is also used in the manufacture of certain kinds of leather, and in the preparation of paints and varnishes. This trade in rock-oil has become very extensive, and is every day becoming more and more highly appreciated as a servant of civilization; the revenue which it produced being of great magnitude, and the number of people which it supports very numerous.

IRON

The next important mineral product that we have to notice is iron, recognized as the most useful known to man. It is more widely distributed throughout the United States than any of the important metals. It is found in abundance in New York, New Hampshire, Massachusetts, Connecticut, Maryland, and Ohio, Michigan, Wisconsin, Oregon, Virginia, the Carolinas, Alabama, and Missouri; but is chiefly mined in Pennsylvania and New Jersey where the yield is more than one-half of the whole product in the United States, or about seven hundred tons per annum, from one hundred and thirty establishments. In Missouri it is found in great abundance, where there is a hill called "Iron Mountain," which is more than two hundred feet high, and is supposed to contain two hundred and fifty millions of tons of pure metal. Another well-nigh solid iron mountain is called "Pilot Knob," nearly six hundred feet high and, it is thought, would furnish one million tons per annum for two hundred years. These two mountains, with another called Shepherd's Mountain, also in Missouri, are considered among the curiosities of America. And yet, with these figures before us, the astounding fact is proclaimed that nearly half a million tons of iron were imported from Great Britain in 1868, while the yield of the United States was about sixteen hundred thousand tons. The fact that there should be any iron imported from England grows out of the operations of the American Tariff. The great magnitude and importance of the iron interest, which can only be fully treated in elaborate volumes, is rendered difficult to notice in a paragraph like the present. The processes by which the ores are turned into metallic iron are as follows: In what are called bloomeries and forges the ores are converted directly into malleable iron, without passing through the intermediate stage of cast or pig iron; and by means of blast-furnaces, the ores are decomposed as they fuse, in vast quantities at a time, and produce the cast or pig iron. Then they have what are called rolling-mills, which convert the iron into sheets and plates. With regard to the uses to which iron is appropriated in the United States, they are well-nigh infinite, and we can only obtain an idea of the extent of its consumption, by reflecting upon the quantity of it which is transferred into steel, for cutlery and machinery; upon the extensive lines of railway in the country and the great number of locomotives employed; and upon manifold uses in connection with shipping and house-building throughout the length and breadth of this immense country.

LEAD

We come now to speak of the production of lead in the United States. The two most prominent deposits of this useful mineral are to be found in the States of Missouri and Illinois. The working of the former was commenced in 1854 and the latter in 1718. The largest supply come from those two States, although it is also found in abundance in Wisconsin and Iowa. The American lead is remarkable for it softness and purity, and although obtained with comparative ease, excepting what is mined in Illinois and Iowa, it is not easily transported to market. The total production of the Union, during the year 1869, was estimated at thirty-eight millions of pounds, while Spain produced about sixty-seven millions, and Great Britain more than one hundred and fifty-three millions of pounds. . . . The uses to which the metal is applied are very numerous and highly important. One of the most useful applications of lead is in the manufacture of the carbonate, which is extensively used as a white paint, and also as a body for other colors. The smelting of lead and the manufacture of the white paint therefrom, are considered prejudicial to health, and the workmen suffer much from colic and paralysis.

QUICKSILVER, ETC.

Another of the more important minerals found in the United States, in almost inexhaustible quantities, is quicksilver. It is chiefly mined in California, where the annual product is considerably more than half the yield of the whole world beside, the total annual yield having been about six hundred thousand pounds. Until recently the mines of Spain controlled the Chinese market, but the miners of California shipped a large amount to Hong Kong, where they sold it far below cost, and the supply from Spain was driven back to that country. The English market is now supplied by Spain and the Chinese market by California. Besides the countries named, Austria and Peru furnish a small supply of this valuable mineral. The chief demand for it is for mining purposes, and for the manufacture of calomel and vermilion.

With regard to the metals known as tin, zinc, platinum, nickel, antimony, cobalt, and other minor metals, they are all found in various parts of the United States, but none of them have as yet been mined to any great extent. With the increase of population and railways, it is supposed that the business of mining will grow into a gigantic national interest, and that America will lead the world in the value and variety of her mineral products. The National Government, within the last few years, has done much to develop the hidden resources of the land, by sending forth competent scientific expeditions, and publishing their results for the benefit of the public; and the people themselves have manifested their interest in the subject by establishing and supporting a number of well-conducted journals devoted wholly to Mining-Engineering.

THE MINERS

In taking a general survey of the mining population of America, we cannot but conclude that they are noted for their intelligence, and, in view of the hardship and privations which they undergo, are not as well paid as they should be, although better paid than the mining people of other countries. A very large proportion of them, however, are foreigners, and as they have generally improved their condition by emigrating to this country, they are contented with their lot. Those of them who are engaged in mining coal, iron, lead, and copper, in the older States of the Union, have facilities for the education of their children at common-schools, but in the frontier States and Territories, where the precious metals are chiefly found, family-men are not abundant, and the opportunities for making them comfortable, and educating the young, are few and far between.

Chapter Ten

Life in the Army and Navy

The standing army of the United States began with the foundation of the Government in 1789, but, when necessary, it has always been customary to employ what is called a volunteer force or army. During the war of the Revolution the number of soldiers employed was 275,000; in the War of 1812, the combined troops numbered 527,631; during the Seminole War of 1817, 5,661; Black Hawk War of 1832, 5,031; Florida War of 1842, 29,953; War with Mexico in 1846, 73,260; miscellaneous troubles, about 20,000; and during the late Civil War, the forces in the field at one time numbered 2,688,523. The total amount of money expended by the United States in carrying on its various wars was $3,308,352,706. . . . [Lengthy passage describing specific numbers of officers and soliders in the army and their ranks, plus regimental divisions circa 1870 has been deleted.]

THE DEPARTMENT WAR

The President is by law Commander-in-Chief of the Armed Forces. To assist him in the execution of the laws, in so far as they relate to the army, in its control, subsistence and supply, a Secretary of War is appointed by him, through whom he exercises as general supervision. To facilitate this a Department of War has been established, which is sub-divided into the following staff departments or corps:

1. Adjutant-General's Department.
2. Inspector-General's Department.
3. Bureau of Military Justice.
4. Quartermaster's Department.

5. Subsistence Department.
6. Medical Department.
7. Pay Department.
8. Signal Office.
9. Chief of Staff to the General of the Army.
10. Corps of Engineers.
11. Ordinance Department.

The general staff is the central point of military administration. It comprises all the officers concerned in regulating the details of the service, and furnishing the army with the means necessary for its subsistence, comfort, mobility, and action.

All general orders which emanate from the headquarters of the army, the orders of detail, of instruction, of movement, and all general regulations for the army, are communicated to the troops through the office of the Adjutant-General.

The Adjutant-General is charged with the record of military appointments, promotions, resignations, deaths, and other casualties; with the registry and filling up of commissions, and with their distribution; with the records which relate to the personnel of the army, and to the military history of every officer and soldier; with the duties connected with the recruiting service; the registry of the names of soldiers; their enlistment and descriptive lists, and of deaths, desertions, discharges, etc.; with the preservation of monthly returns of regiments and posts, and the muster-rolls of companies; with receipts and examination of applications for pension, previous to their being sent to the Pension Office, and of inventories of the effects of deceased soldiers.

The annual returns of the militia of the several States and Territories; of the ordnance, arms, accoutrements, and munitions of war appertaining to the same, required by law to be made to the President of the United States, are filed, and the general returns of the militia annually required to be laid before Congress, are also prepared and consolidated in this office.

The Inspector-General's Department is charged with the duty of inspecting and reporting upon the condition of the forts, with their armaments, of the state of discipline of the troops—in short, upon the whole "material and personnel" of the army, and to report whether or not the prescribed rules, regulations, and orders for its government are properly carried into effect.

In the office of the Judge Advocate-General, under whose charge is the Bureau of Military Justice, the proceedings of all courts-martial, courts of inquiry, and military commissions, are received, revised, recorded, and reported upon. It is the duty of the Judge Advocate-General to report at once for the action of the Secretary of War, all fatal irregularities in proceedings and illegal or unusual sentences. When called upon by the proper authority, he gives an opinion on questions of construction of military law; and through him all communications pertaining to questions of military justice should be addressed.

The Quartermaster-General's Department furnishes to the army its transportation, of whatever nature, quarters, fuel, stationery, etc., and pays for rent of quarters and for all materials to be used in the construction of buildings for its use. To that office are sent all reports and returns of property purchased, issued, worn out in service, lost, sold, destroyed, or remaining on hand, and there are approved all contracts for purchases connected with the above.

The Subsistence Department, as its name implies, has charge of the furnishing of subsistence to troops. All reports and returns necessary to the end that stores may be properly accounted for are made to this office, and here all contracts for their purchase are approved.

The Medical Department, or Surgeon-General's Office, has charge of the selection of medical offices for detail, and to it all returns and reports in regard to sick and wounded officers and soldiers, and medical stores, are made. With regard to the other bureaus or offices which have been mentioned, their duties are described by their titles.

We may further remark, in brief, that the American army is divided into divisions and departments commanded by generals. [I]n times of peace it is chiefly employed in occupying the various forts and defenses of the country, and in keeping peace with the Indians on the frontiers. After forty years of service, the officers of the army may at their own request be retired, receiving seventy five percent of their pay. Members of Congress designate the largest proportion of those who are admitted to the West Point Academy, which is the regular school for the education of officers for the army. When, in time of war, it is necessary to have volunteers, they are called for by proclamation of the President, and the State governors immediately answer the call, and send the proportion assigned to them, which are chiefly composed of the militia or State troops. After the war, these volunteer troops are disbanded and return to the ordinary avocations of life, which fact has been considered by foreigners as one of the marvels of the American Government. The regular army is supplied with soldiers by enlistment, and after entering the service, no man can leave it without the consent of Government, nor without sufficient cause. With regard to the pay of the army, which is always enhanced by long service, we submit the following: general $13,500; lieutenant-general, $11,000; major-general, $7,500; brigadier-general, $5,500; colonel, $3,500; lieutenant-colonel, $3,000; major, $2,500; captains, $1,800 and $2,000; regimental adjutant and quartermaster, each $1,800; first lieutenants, $1,500 and $1,600; second lieutenants, $1,400 and $1,500; and chaplains, $1,500. The pay of the common soldier is $13 per month, with rations. There are 25 armories and arsenals in the country, all in command of competent officers, and the Military Departments of the Government number 15, and embrace the whole Union. The amount required for supporting the military establishments during 1872 is about $29,000,000.

THE NAVY

As the War Department is the centre of the army, so is the Navy Department the fountain head of the navy. The duties of this department are distributed through the Secretary's office and eight bureaus: [1] Bureau of Yards and Docks, which has charge of the navy-yards, including the docks, wharves, buildings, and machinery, and also of a Naval Asylum; [2] Office of Navigation, which has charge of the maps, charts, flags, signals, etc., and also of the Naval Academy, Naval Observatory, and Nautical Almanac; [3] Office of Ordnance, which has charge of ordnance and ordnance stores, the manufacture and purchase of cannon, guns, powder, shot, shell, etc.; [4] Office of Construction and Repair, having charge of the construction of vessels of war; [5] Office of Equipment and Recruiting, which has charge of the enlistment of men for the navy, the equipment of vessels, anchors, cables, rigging, sails, coal, etc.; [6] Office of Provisions and Clothing; [7] Office of Steam Engineering; and [8] Office of Medicine and Surgery—the duties of which last two are described by their titles. There is attached to the Navy Department what is called the Marine Corps, whose duties are allied to those of the army, only that they are performed on board ship or at the navy-yard. [There is] also a National Observatory, which has earned a world-wide reputation; and a Hydrographic Office, which, with the observatory, annually publishes volumes of scientific information of great value.

The largest vessel in the United States Navy has a displacement of 55,440 feet, carries 12 guns, and, like the majority in the service, is a screw steamer. Some other ships, however, carry 45 guns. Of those ranking as first-rates there are 5; second-rates, 40; third-rates, 43; fourth-rates, 10; to which may be added the iron-clads, receiving and practice ships, supply vessels and tugs, making in all 179, and carrying in the aggregate 1,390 guns. The officers of the navy, to which we affix their "at sea" salaries, are as follows: 1 admiral, $13,000; 1 vice-admiral, $9,000; 12 rear-admirals, $6,000; 24 commodores, $5,000; 50 captains, $4,500; 89 commanders, $3,500; 164 lieutenant-commanders, $2,800; 201 lieutenants, $2,400; 75 masters, $1,800; 68 ensigns, $1,200; 113 midshipmen, $1,000; 150 in Medical Corps, whose salaries are widely various; 1134 in the Pay Corps, with various salaries; and 241 in the Engineer Corps, together with an ample supply of naval constructors, chaplains, professors of mathematics, and civil engineers, who salaries range from $1,700 to $4,400, and are increased with length of service. The pay of common seamen is $21.50 per month, and while the subordinate grades in the service number 57, their pay ranges from $8 to $456 per month. The academy where young men are fitted for service in the navy is located at Annapolis, and is under rules, in regard to admission, allied to those of the military Academy at West Point. Of complete navy-yards there are eight in the United States; five fleets are now doing duty in various quarters of the globe; and within the last year several scientific expeditions have been fitted out as follows: One to survey the Isthmus of Tehuantepec and another to survey the Isthmus of Darien, both of which have in view the making of a canal between the Atlantic and Pacific Oceans; and an expedition has also been fitted out for explorations towards the North Pole. Indirectly connected with the navy is a bureau called the Light-House Board, with which, as an active member, has hitherto been connected to Admiral Thornton A. Jenkins, but who has recently been assigned to the fleet in the waters of China and Japan. Without going more fully into the subject for want of space it only remains for us to add in conclusion, that the sum of money which will be required to support the American naval establishment during the year 1872 will be about $20,000,000.

Chapter Eleven

Life in the Leading Cities

The total number of incorporated cities in the United States is 409, but many of them do not contain more than 2,000 inhabitants.

NEW YORK CITY

By far the largest proportion of foreigners who come to this country across the Atlantic Ocean enter the country at the port of New York, which is the largest city in the Western Hemisphere. It was founded by the Dutch, and called by them New Amsterdam. It occupies the greater part of an island called Manhattan, which is 13½ miles long, and contains an area of 22 miles. The cities of Brooklyn and Jersey City, and several other towns, although having each a government of their own, are in reality portions of New York, and their combined population is not far from 11,500,000. According to the last census, the population of New York by itself was 942,292; of whom 523,198 were born in the United States, and 484,109 in the State of New York. Within eight miles of the commercial metropolis, in New Jersey, is a city called Newark, [having a population] of 100,000 people. But it is so closely identified with the former in its business and social interests as almost to be considered a suburb of New York. During the last fifteen years the number of immigrants arriving there from various parts of the world was about 2,341,000; the arrivals for 1870 alone having been 211,190, and it is estimated that about four-fifths of these foreigners found permanent homes in the various States of the interior.

The principal street of New York, which runs through its entire length like a backbone, is called Broadway, and for several miles is completely lined with iron and marble buildings, devoted chiefly to business pursuits, and winning for it the reputation of being one of the handsomest and wealthiest streets in the world. But much of this splendor is also found in all its subordinate streets and avenues where the houses are generally built of brick. And, as a street for private residences, Fifth Avenue is claimed to be unsurpassed. Projecting, as this city does, into a splendid harbor, where the fortifications are strong and imposing, it is perpetually surrounded with a forest of shipping, which gives the stranger an adequate idea of its very extensive commerce. The value of its real and personal estate has not been definitely settled, but has been estimated at nearly $800,000,000, and the rate of taxation is 2 percent per annum. It is supplied with pure water by an aqueduct which cost more than $15,000,000, the water-pipes of which measure some 270 miles. It has 100 miles of sewers, and more than 200 miles of paved streets. Its temples for religious worship are numerous, and many of them very beautiful; the church property of the city reaching in value nearly $115,000,000.

Its principal park, known as Central Park, is said to be equal to the best in Europe, and its principal financial street, known as Wall Street, although not more than half a mile in length, has a power which is felt in the remotest corners of the earth. Its hospitals and other benevolent institutions are numerous and liberally conducted in every particular, and the same may be said of its institutions of learning, ranging from first-class colleges to the best of district or common schools. It is abundantly supplied with libraries, many of which are very large, and all of them are conducted on the most liberal principles. Its manufacturing establishments are numberless. Its fire department is noted for its efficiency, and is founded on the voluntary system. And there is a lively military spirit among its young men; its militia regiments rival veteran regulars in their drill. Its police force is of the first order and is managed by commissioners. Policemen are appointed during good behavior, and officers rise from the ranks. . . . There are about 700 police stations, 412 miles of streets, and 11 miles of piers in the city.

Its newspapers are abundant and, taken in the aggregate, are probably more influential for good or evil than any similar number on the globe. Its markets for the necessaries of life are fully supplied with everything that can be desired in the way of meats, flour, fruit, and fish. Its government, although resting upon the most liberal provisions, has for many years been a kind of political arena, in which unworthy men have obtained and exercised the most dangerous powers, and at the moment of writing these lines, a number of men who were lately at the head of the city government are confined in a common prison for robbing their fellow-citizens to an enormous extent. While it is true that New York is very much of a cosmopolitan city, it has been estimated that two-thirds of its inhabitants are natives of the United States. It is, however, pre-eminently a commercial city, and in several respects is equal to London. The Post-Office of New York is the most important in the country; and its customs receipts amount to about three-fifths of the total in the United States. The manufactures of the city constitute a leading element of its prosperity and wealth. The most numerous class of workmen are those engaged in making wearing apparel; next to whom come the workmen in fibrous substances, glass, and pottery, and the manufacturers of cars and wagons. . . . Nowhere is the habit of eating away from home so general as in New York, owing to the great distance between the dwelling-houses and the places of business; and this habit has made eating-houses, lunch-rooms, refectories, oyster-cellars, and bar-rooms, a prominent feature of the place. Its hotels are quite magnificent, and its boarding-houses as comfortable as any in the world. The eating-houses are found everywhere, and are frequented by the millionaire as well as the vagabond. The city government is vested in a Mayor and Boards of Aldermen and Councilmen, who are annually elected by the people. While it is true that in times of high political excitement it is sometimes afflicted with mobs and riots, the din of business always ceases on the approach of the Sabbath, and that day is observed as a day of rest, of church-going, and of recreation, by its teeming thousands. The spring and autumn are the two great seasons for business; winter, the special season for amusements and all sorts of gaiety; while the summer is comparatively sluggish, although, even then, the turmoil of business is far from being dead.

PHILADELPHIA

The second largest city in the United States is Philadelphia, which was founded by William Penn in 1682, and contains 674,022 inhabitants, of whom 490,398 were born in the United States, and 428,250 in Pennsylvania. It stands on a plain between the rivers Delaware and Schuylkill, and has several suburban cities, the whole of which form one municipality containing 120 square miles. The streets of the city proper are laid out in regular order, and the houses are more distinguished for their neatness and comfort than for their richness or extravagance, and in this particular are in keeping with the character of the population. The city is well supplied with parks, one of which, with its collection of trees and scenes of beauty, is considered a successful rival of the great Central Park of New York. Its public buildings are numerous and beautiful. One of them, called Girard College, was built and the institution endowed by one of its citizens alone. But the chief boast of the inhabitants is Independence Hall, which was the meeting-place of Congress during the earlier history of the American Republic. The churches are also numerous, all the religious denominations being well supplied, but this is especially the case in regard to the Quakers who have hitherto been so numerous and influential as to have given to their city the name of *Quaker City*. The literary and scientific institutions of Philadelphia have always occupied a high position, and the cultured character of its inhabitants has always been manifested by its rich libraries and galleries of art, and by the upright character of its press. It was here that Benjamin Franklin lived and worked as a printer, and won his great fame as a philosopher. From the earliest times the central mint of the United States has been established here, and the city has borne an important part in the financial history of the country. Because of its remoteness from the Atlantic Ocean it may not compete with New York in its foreign commerce, but it carries on an immense trade with the interior country, and is a noted terminus for unnumbered railroads and canals. As a depot for the exportation of coal it is without a rival, and it has always been famous for the extent of its book-publishing business.

Within the last few years Philadelphia has greatly increased its manufacturing establishments, until its inhabitants now claim that they can produce everything that may be required for the comfort or convenience of man. Indeed, in the variety and extent of its manufactures it is said to be unequalled by any other city in the Union. On this point, we submit one illustration, which is that it contains the two largest establishments in the world for the manufacture of locomotives, which give employment to about 4,000 hands, and can build one of those wonderful engines in a single day. . . . While the inhabitants of this city are noted for their peaceful disposition and for their love of order, it is also true that it has been the scene of many political or religious disturbances, but which in these latter days have been quite unknown. Another of the characteristics of this city is the total absence of tenement houses, and the existence of comfortable homes for the laboring population. As one of her public men informs us, every laborer who has a family . . . [dwells] in a house lighted by gas, and supplied with an abundance of pure water. As this city is pre-eminently a producing city, so are its native and foreign inhabitants distinguished for their industry, and there is not in the whole land, probably, any other crowded city where among the working classes more genuine comfort and contentment can be found.

BOSTON

The next city on our list is Boston, which contains 250,526 inhabitants, of whom 172,450 were born in the United States and 127,620 in the State of Massachusetts. If we should add to it the various towns which adjoin it, the population would be nearly double. It was first settled in 1630 by the Puritans, and is the leading city of New England, upon which it has always exerted a paramount influence. It bore a very important part in the history of the American Revolution, and events of great importance have transpired within its limits and in its vicinity. Formerly it was more closely identified with the commerce of the East [i.e., Asia] than any other American city, and at the present time ranks next to New York in the extent of its foreign commerce. The city is chiefly situated on a peninsula, and some of the adjacent parts, with which it is connected by numerous bridges, rise to the height of one hundred and thirty feet above the level of the harbor, which is deep, convenient, and·secure. The streets were originally laid out upon no systematic plan, and being accommodated to the unevenness of the surface, many of them are crooked and narrow, but these defects are being annually remedied. Many of the public buildings are handsome but some of them are more famous for their associations than their imposing appearance. The State House occupies the apex of the city and presents a commanding view of the sea and surrounding country. Its Faneuil Hall is universally known as the "Cradle of Liberty" because it was here that the orators of the Revolution fired the hearts of the people against England. One of its leading land-marks is the monument of Bunker Hill, where was fought a famous battle [on June 17, 1775]. Its wharves and warehouses are on a scale of magnitude surpassed by no other city of the same size. Its churches are numerous, and many of them beautiful, the largest number of them belonging to the Unitarian denomination. It has an extensive park called "Boston Common," which is a delightful resort for the inhabitants during the vernal months.

With regard to literary, scientific, and educational institutions, the city is most abundantly supplied. Its schools have a high reputation, and it published more than one hundred periodicals. Among its many libraries is one, the largest, which is entirely free to all who may desire to enjoy its advantages. The fact that the famous Harvard University is located in one of its suburbs, called Cambridge, has greatly tended to give [Boston] its high reputation as a seat of learning. Its benevolent institutions are also numerous and richly endowed, and it has taken a prominent part in providing for the wants and intellectual elevation of the blind and the comforts of the insane. Its infirmaries have always borne a high reputation. The ice-trade is a Boston invention, and is said to have secured for it the important trade which it enjoys with Calcutta, and other portions of the East. On the score of enterprise and culture, the inhabitants of Boston have no superiors, and that circumstance has tended to make them somewhat clannish or exclusive in their manners and conversation, and their modes of doing business. Hence it is that the outside world, especially the cosmopolitan citizens of New York, occasionally indulge in a little ridicule at the expense of the

Bostonians. It is a thriving city, and, by means of seven or eight great lines of railway, carried on an important trade in manufactures with the interior country. It is a poor place for idlers and beggars, and yet the most liberal provision is made for the deserving poor. While this city does much to promote the fine arts, it claims a reputation of its own for what it has done in developing the arts and music, and it boasts of a church organ which is the largest in the world.

BALTIMORE

Another of the leading cities of America is Baltimore, which has a population of 267,354, of whom 210,870 were born in the United States, and 187,650 in the State of Maryland. It was founded by the Roman Catholics in 1720; is admirably situated both for foreign and internal trade, having a spacious and secure harbor, and occupying a central position as regards the Atlantic coast of the United States. The site of the city is picturesque, covering a number of eminences, and although connected with the Northern and Western States by its business ramifications, it has hitherto been considered a representative of the Southern States. It was here that the first gun was fired by a mob at the commencement of the late Civil War, when a regiment of troops from Massachusetts was assaulted on their way to Washington. Its proximity to the seat of government, from which it is only thirty-eight miles distant, has added to its importance and made it popular with the officials of the nation. From the number and prominence of its monuments, it has been called the "Monumental City." The most imposing of these is surmounted by a statue of George Washington, which stands 312 feet above the adjacent harbor. The city contains a shot-tower which is 250 feet high—the highest in the world. The churches of this city are numerous, and many of them beautiful and imposing. And it boasts of one large park, which is remarkable for the beauty of its scenery and is a successful rival of those in New York and Boston. The manufacturing facilities of Baltimore are uncommon and quite equal to its commercial advantages. In its benevolent and educational institutions it is behind none of its sister cities, and its name is associated with many men of culture, connected with literature, science, and the fine arts. It was here that the famous George Peabody first established himself in business, and where he founded one of the largest educational institutions associated with his name.[1]

---

1. George Peabody (1795–1869), successful businessman and one of America's first philanthropists. Among the many educational institutions that he established are the Peabody Institute, affiliated with Johns Hopkins University in Baltimore, Md., and the Peabody Museum at Harvard University, Cambridge, Mass., and the Peabody Essex Museum in Salem, Mass.

NEW ORLEANS

Among the representative cities of America is New Orleans. It was founded by the French in 1717 and has a population of 191,418. Its site is on the eastern bank of the great Mississippi River, about 100 miles above the mouth of that stream, and as it forms a half circle, has been called the Crescent City. Many parts of it are so low and flat that the waters are kept from overflowing it only by artificial embankments. It possesses unrivalled natural advantages for internal trade, and it is visited by vessels from every quarter of the globe. Every description of craft is employed in transporting to it the rich products of the Mississippi and its many tributaries whose navigable waters are not less than 15,000 miles in extent, and embrace every variety of climate. Not only is it the receptacle of countless varieties of produce from the interior, but is considered the largest cotton market in the world. The particular spot where all this merchandise is received, and from which it is shipped to foreign ports, is called the levee; it extends along the river for miles, and because of the strange co-mingling of ships and steamboats and other kinds of vessels, and also on account of its vast proportions and never-ceasing bustle, has been pronounced by travellers one of the wonders of America. It abounds in handsome buildings, and its various public institutions rest on liberal foundations. On account of its low situation and warm climate it is subject to annual visitations from the yellow fever, which is frequently fatal to strangers. Any description of this city would be incomplete without a notice of its cemeteries. Each one is inclosed with a thick brick wall of arched cavities, made just large enough to admit a single coffin, and rising to the height of twelve feet. Within the enclosure are crowded the tombs, which are built wholly above the ground, and are from one to three stories high. This method of sepulture is a necessity, for the earth is so universally saturated with water, that none but paupers are consigned to the earth. The population of the city is exceedingly varied. Its chief resident inhabitants are known as Creoles—or the native population—and those who are engaged in mercantile pursuits, and are successful, usually remain there during the winter or business months, spending their summers among the highlands of the interior country. It is also thickly inhabited by colored people who were once in slavery. It was the scene of quite a famous battle in 1815 between the English and the Americans under Andrew Jackson, who was victorious, and subsequently became President of the United States. The prevailing religion is Roman Catholic, and many churches are modelled upon those of European countries. Notwithstanding the fact that this city is sometimes called the "West Grave," and the "City of the Dead," it is celebrated for its continuous round of gayeties, from the beginning of the year to its close.

ST. LOUIS

On leaving New Orleans, if we pass up the Mississippi River about 1,200 miles, we come to the city of St. Louis, which contains 310,864 inhabitants. It was founded by the French fur-traders, and possesses the peculiarity of being located at the geographical centre of the North American Continent. Its advantages as a commercial emporium are probably not surpassed by those of any inland port in the world. The business transacted here by means of steamboats and railroads is enormous; the people are cosmopolitan in their character, and not behind the cities of the Eastern States in their industry, liberality, and intellectual culture. And what we say of St. Louis is also true of Cincinnati, on the Ohio, with its 216,239 inhabitants; of Louisville, on the same river, with its 100,753 inhabitants; and of Chicago, on Lake Michigan.

THE CHICAGO FIRE

With regard to the last named place, we may remark that its rapid growth in 25 years, from a village to a city of nearly 300,000, is one of the marvels of the age. But, since the first pages of this volume were sent to press, Chicago has met with a calamity by fire, which has been pronounced quite unprecedented. It occurred in October 1871, and resulted in the total destruction of all the business portions of the city. More than 100 lives were also lost, 80,000 persons, including merchants and mechanics, were thrown out of employment or reduced to beggary in a single night, and the total loss of property was estimated at $200,000,000. It is said to have been the most extensive fire that ever occurred in any country, and the sympathy felt for the sufferers called forth subscriptions of money from every quarter of the globe, amounting in the aggregate to many millions of dollars. What was still more wonderful was the fact that the regular business of the city was again in successful operation in a very few weeks, although it had to be transacted under many and great disadvantages.

SAN FRANCISCO

Having elsewhere touched upon the characteristics of Washington, the metropolis of the United States, with its 120,000 inhabitants, we conclude our list of the larger cities with an allusion to San Francisco, which contains about 150,000 inhabitants. The rapidity of its growth can only be compared with that of Chicago; and while the former was chiefly built up by the gold mines of California, the latter owes its prosperity to the agricultural development of the wide and fertile region of which it is the centre. The fact that San Francisco is the largest American seaport on the Pacific Ocean, and that it is at the terminus of the Pacific Railroad, gives it command of the commerce of all the Eastern nations, by which advantages it will probably become a city of vast importance and influence. From the nature of its position, its social characteristics are quite different from those of the Atlantic cities, and it is not behind them in any of those qualities which give power and dignity to a city; yet it stands quite alone in regard to its Chinese population.[2] The high rates of labor in this city generally, and its dependence on importation for all its iron, brass, cotton, hardware, and most of its wool, leather, and hard-wood lumber, prevent the establishment of factories, and all the cutlery, fine tools, and machinery, glass, porcelain, clothing, and shoes are necessarily obtained from abroad at a great expense, thus giving employment to a large amount of shipping.

CITIES WITH LESS THAN 100,000 PEOPLE

In our remarks thus far, we have only spoken of those American cities which contain more than 100,000 inhabitants. But there are many smaller cities, which have a world-wide fame on account of their beauty, business characteristics, or historical associations. Among these may be mentioned Charleston, which has about 50,000 inhabitants, is the centre of the rice-producing country of South Carolina, and in whose harbor at Fort Sumter, was made the first regular assault upon the national forces at the commencement of the late Civil War when the city was a great sufferer. Savannah, the chief seaport of Georgia and the rival of Charleston, having a population of nearly 30,000. Richmond, in Virginia, with more than 50,000 inhabitants, and famous for its beautiful location, its flour and tobacco trade, and for having been the headquarters of the late rebellion. Mobile, in Alabama, with 32,000 inhabitants, possessing characteristics similar to those of New Orleans. Detroit, in Michigan, with nearly 80,000 inhabitants, beautiful for situation, and the commercial gateway to the Great Lakes of Huron, Michigan, and Superior. Milwaukee, in Wisconsin, with 71,000 inhabitants, the counterpart of Chicago, and its unsuccessful rival. Cleveland, in Ohio, with 93,000 energetic inhabitants. Buffalo, at the eastern end of Lake Erie, with a population of 115,000 souls—near which are the Falls of Niagara. Pittsburgh, in Pennsylvania, with a population of 86,000, almost entirely devoted to the coal and

---

2. San Francisco had the largest Chinese immigrant population of any city in the United States.

iron interests. Albany, in New York, the head of navigation on the Hudson, and famous for its Dutch history, and as being the Capital of the Empire State, with 70,000 people. Rochester and Troy, in the same State, with 63,000 souls. Indianapolis, in Indiana, with 48,000 people, and famous for its surrounding agricultural country. Portland, in Maine, which has 32,000 souls, and one of the best harbors in America. And the cities of Cambridge, in Massachusetts, and New Haven, in Connecticut, where are located two of the leading colleges of the United States.[3]

---

3. Harvard University, in Cambridge Mass., and Yale University, in New Haven Conn.

Chapter Twelve

Frontier Life and Developments

The frontiers of America are so extensive, and the pursuits of their inhabitants so various, that an entire volume would not suffice to describe them with minuteness. In taking a bird's-eye view of the domain in question . . . we propose to speak of the four following characteristics: the Indians, the Pioneer Farmers, the Fur-Traders and Trappers, and the Lumbermen.

THE INDIANS OF NORTH AMERICA

It is now a settled fact that the Red race, or native Indians of America, are gradually passing away under the march of civilization. According to the most authentic data, the number of Indians who recognize the President as their Great Father is about 300,000. Of these, the Creeks, Cherokees, Choctaws, and Chickasaws, who live on the head-waters of the Arkansas, number some 54,000; and, excepting 4,000 of the Six Nations in New York, 1,000 Cherokees in North Carolina, 600 Penobscots in Maine, and 41,000 of various tribes still holding reservations on the Great Lakes, and the Mississippi and Missouri Rivers. [These] are the only tribes that have made any satisfactory advances in acquiring the arts and comforts of civilization. It would thus appear that the number of wild Indians who live entirely by the chase, and inhabit the American territories, excluding Alaska, number 200,000 souls. Although nominally obedient to the laws of the United States, these hunting tribes are, in reality, as free to roam as if there were no central government. But with those who are partially civilized the case is quite different. Their wealth has been estimated at $3,300,000, while they support about 70 schools, nearly the same number of teachers or missionaries, and cultivate nearly 1,000 acres of land. The names by which they are known number 150, and their geographical condition is co-extensive with the area of the United States and Territories. It is a remarkable fact, that of all the races or classes of people who inhabit the United States, the Indians are the only people who are not recognized as citizens by the General Government.

On leaving the hunting-grounds of the Red Men for the haunts of opening civilization, the first thing which attracts attention is the cabin of the pioneer or frontier farmer. Though born and bred in a settled country, this man, who represents a large class, has been tempted by the spirit of enterprise to purchase a few hundred acres of land at the low government price, which he is clearing away as rapidly as possible, and in the midst of which he has fixed his home. It is built of logs, small, and poorly furnished, and but for the smoke issuing from its rustic chimney, could hardly be distinguished from the stable or barn where he shelters his horses and oxen and cows. Hard work and rough fare are the lot of this poor yeoman, but his mission . . . commands the highest respect. He has a growing family about him, and in their welfare are centred all his hopes. Though far removed from schools and churches and the refinements of life, he plods on year after year, giving his boys the best education he can, thankful that they are approaching man's estate, and cheered with the prospect that, like many of his predecessors in a new country, he will acquire a fortune and spend his old age in a large frame or brick house and end his days in peace. Five, ten, or it may be fifteen miles from this man's cabin is another, built on the same model, and whose owner is a counterpart of himself. Farther on, still another log-cabin comes in view, and so on do they continue to appear, encompassing the entire frontiers of civilization. The ancestors of many of these men were among those who originally fought on the battlefield for the independence of their country, and they themselves, with their brothers and sons, flocked by thousands to its rescue, during the late Civil War in America. These men embody the true spirit of the land in which they dwell, and in history they will be long remembered with honor and gratitude for what they have done to make clear the pathway of empire.

FUR TRADERS AND TRAPPERS

We come now to speak of that class of people living on the frontiers known as fur-traders and trappers. The business of collecting and selling furs and peltries was commenced immediately after the first settlement of the country, and for about two hundred years was eminently lucrative, and gave employment to the large numbers of enterprising men. Representatives from France and England, as well as the United States, participated in the trade, and several companies of great magnitude and influence were the outgrowth of this trade, such as the Hudson's Bay Company, the Northwest Company, and the American Fur Company. Of late years, however, the fur business has greatly declined on the American Continent, but is not yet extinct. The men called traders are those who locate themselves on the borders of the wilderness, and keep for sale ample supplies of all such articles as may be needed by the Indians or trappers, who pay for what they purchase with furs and peltries. The more common articles required are blankets, guns and ammunition, flour and pork, tobacco, knives, as well as trinkets and the baneful fire-water, while the articles for which they are exchanged are buffalo robes, and the skins of the deer, the beaver, and the otter, the sable, the mink, the bear, and the wolf, for all of which there is always a demand in the cities of the Atlantic States. The men known as trappers are either white men or half-breeds (so called, because they are the offspring of French fathers and Indian mothers), and they are the successful rivals of the native Indians in hunting or trapping wild animals. Those who reside in the prairie countries or among the Rocky Mountains chiefly employ the bark-canoe in their operations. In the earlier times, when America was yet a wilderness, this latter class of men rendered important service to the English and French nations, by acting as guides and assistants in the exploring expeditions, and they became universally known as *voyageurs*. While there are many American towns and cities which owe their origin to the existence of the fur-trade, the two most noted of these are St. Louis, on the Mississippi River, and Montreal, in Canada, which lies on the river St. Lawrence, but both of these noted cities are rapidly losing their former reputations, and have really become cosmopolitan in their character, as well as cities of great magnitude and importance in the history of commerce.

LUMBERMEN

But by far the most important phase of frontier life in the United States is that connected with the lumbering business. There is no country on the globe which equals America in the extent of its valuable forests, and there is a great and constantly increasing demand for every variety of lumber, for the building of houses and the countless other things which are made of wood and indispensable for the comfort of mankind. The manufacture of lumber is of the utmost importance, and is a prominent source of wealth in America. The aggregate value of the trade amount[s] to more than one hundred millions of dollars, and giv[es] employment to nearly one hundred thousand persons in its various departments. The variety of forest-trees which are cut down and transformed into lumber is very great, but the pine is most abundant, next to which may be mentioned the fir, spruce, and hemlock, all of which are found in the Eastern, Northern, and Northwestern States. The various marketable articles which are manufactured out of these several woods are known as timber, staves, shingles, boards of every thickness, scantling, masts and knees for shipping; and the uses to which these productions are applied are endless, and of vast importance to the people in every sphere of life. In North Carolina they have a peculiar kind of pine, which they not only manufacture into lumber, but from which the inhabitants obtain large quantities of tar, pitch, and turpentine. In Alabama and Mississippi they have still another variety of pine, which is worked into spars and masts by the ship-builders of the country. In Florida, an extensive business is done in preparing the live oak of that region for use in building the naval vessels of the country—the Government retaining the monopoly of that valuable product. In many of the Western States there is a tree called the black walnut, which is employed to a great extent in the manufacture of elegant furniture, and has competed successfully with the imported wood called mahogany.

With regard to the various classes of people engaged in the lumbering business throughout the Union, the most numerous are called lumbermen. In all those regions where the white pine and spruce and fir prevail, they form extensive parties, and spend the winter in the dense forests, cutting down trees and dragging the logs to the banks of the streams; and when spring comes, and the streams become full of water, they drive the logs down the rivers, and in immense quantities, all arranged in rafts, deliver them at the saw-mills at the mouths of the streams and on navigable waters, where the logs are turned into all kinds of lumber, and thence shipping by vessels to various parts of the United States as well as to foreign countries. Many of the merchants or companies who employ these lumbermen do business on a scale of great magnitude, and they not only control the various operations in the interior, but are also the owners of the mills where the lumber is made, as well as many of the vessels employed in the carrying-trade. The mills to which we have alluded are generally so located as to be driven by water-power, and as they are very numerous and extensive, they give employment to workmen of many grades who form a class quite distinct from that of lumbermen. They are for the most part an intelligent and hardy race of men, and fail not, when elections take place, to exert an important influence on the affairs of their own State or those of the General Government.

As we pass into the pine forests of Carolina, we there find another state of affairs. In that region, the manufacture of lumber is carried on in conjunction with the production of tar, pitch, and turpentine, and by far the largest proportion of the men employed were formerly the colored people called slaves, but now known as Freedmen. There, as well as elsewhere, the prevailing business is conducted by organized companies or by men of ample means, who give employment, and a good support, to large numbers of hard-working men. Those who live in the States bordering on the Gulf of Mexico, especially in Florida, and who prepare the live-oak timber for the use at the navy-yards, are mostly men from the north, with northern habits and constitutions, and are exclusively employed by the General Government. They also pursue their arduous labors in the winter-months, and, like the lumbermen of New England, live in tents or cabins, and on the plainest fare. As to the business of spar-cutting in Alabama and Mississippi, it requires so little sagacity, that it is chiefly carried on by those who own the forest-lands. But when we pass on to the Northwestern States, where the black walnut prevails, we find the business of lumbering fully organized, and the durable and rich-looking wood carefully prepared for transportation by steamboats or railroads to the markets on the Atlantic coast. There is also an extensive lumber business done in the Pacific States and Territories, and the "big trees" of California have obtained a world-wide reputation.

Chapter Thirteen

Judicial Life

The Constitution provides that, "the judicial power of the United States shall be vested in one Supreme Court, and in such inferior courts as the Congress may from time to time ordain and establish." The Constitution further defines and limits the judicial power as follows [in Article III, Section 2]:

1. The judicial power shall extend to all cases, in law and equity, arising under this Constitution, the laws of the United States, and treaties made, or which shall be made, under their authority; to all cases affecting ambassadors, other public ministers, and consuls; to all cases of admiralty and maritime jurisdiction; to controversies to which the United States shall be a party; to controversies between two or more States, between a State and citizens of another State, between citizens of different States, between citizens of the same State claiming lands under grants of different States, and between a State or the citizens thereof and foreign states, citizens, or subjects.

2. In all cases affecting ambassadors, other public ministers and consuls, and those in which a state shall be a party, the Supreme Court shall have original jurisdiction. In all the other cases before mentioned, the Supreme Court shall have appellate jurisdiction both as to law and fact, with such exceptions, and under such regulations as the Congress shall make.

The Supreme Court being established by the Constitution, Congress has from time to time established the following additional "inferior courts" of the United States: The Circuit Courts, the District Courts, the Court of Claims, the Supreme Court of the District of Columbia, the Territorial Courts, with the Supreme Court, constitute the Judiciary of the United States. The outlines of their powers, jurisdiction, etc., will be briefly presented as follows:

I. The Supreme Court. The original jurisdiction of the Supreme Court is defined in the Constitution, as quoted [above]. Its appellate jurisdiction is also there defined, but is provided to be subject to exceptions and regulation by Congress. This power Congress has exercised in the following instances. Appeals from these Circuit Courts to the Supreme Court, in civil actions, equity cases, and admiralty and prize cases, are restricted to those in which the matter in dispute exceeds the sum or value of two thousand dollars, exclusive of costs. But this restriction does not apply to patent, copyright or revenue cases; nor does it affect appeals in criminal cases. Congress has also provided that the Supreme Court shall have appellate jurisdiction from judgments or decrees of the highest courts of the several States in suits . . . [which] question the validity of a treaty or statute of, or an authority exercised under, the United States, and the decision has been against their validity; or where is drawn in question the validity of a statute or an authority exercised under any State on the ground of their being repugnant to the Constitution, treaties, or laws of the United States, and the decision is in favor of such validity; or where any title, right, privilege, or immunity is claimed under the Constitution, treaties, or laws of the United States, and the decision is against the title, rights, etc. But from the operations of these provisions are excepted cases of persons held in the custody of the military authorities of the United States, charged with military offences, or with having aided or abetted rebellion against the Government.

The Supreme Court sits at Washington, and holds one annual session, commencing on the first Monday in December,[1] with such adjourned or special terms as may be found necessary for the despatch of business. It consists of a Chief Justice and eight Justices who, in common with all the United States [federal] judges, hold their offices during good behavior.[2] The salary of the Chief Justice is eight thousand five hundred dollars; that of each of the Justices eight thousand dollars per annum. Six of the nine constitute a quorum.

II. The Circuit Courts are nine in number; the United States being divided into nine circuits, each comprising three or more districts. Justices of the Supreme Court are allotted by that Court to the several circuits [i.e., one to each of the nine circuits], to assist in holding the Circuit Courts. Each circuit has a Circuit Judge with a salary of six thousand dollars; with the same power and jurisdiction as the Justice of the Supreme Court allotted to the circuit. The Circuit Court in each circuit is held by the Justice of the Supreme Court, or by the Circuit Judge of the circuit, or by the District Judge of the district—sitting alone; or by the Justice of the Supreme Court and Circuit Judge sitting together; or (in the absence of either of them) by the other and the district judge. Where two judges hold a Circuit Court, and differ in opinion, the law provides

---

1. Later changed to the first Monday in October.
2. Usually for the rest of one's lifetime or voluntary retirement.

for a special appeal to the Supreme Court. There are two annual sessions of each Circuit Court, with special sessions for the trial of criminal cases. The jurisdiction of the Circuit Courts is as follows: They have concurrent jurisdiction, with the State Courts, of civil suits at common law and equity, where the matter in dispute exceeds, exclusive of costs, the sum or value of five hundred dollars, and where the United States are plaintiffs or petitioners, or an alien is a party (but not where both parties are aliens); or where the suit is between a citizen of the State in which the suit is brought, and a citizen of another State. They have exclusive jurisdiction of all crimes and offences cognizable under the authority of the United States, except of such as are within the jurisdiction of the District Courts, and of those they have concurrent jurisdiction. They have also original jurisdiction in all patent and copyright cases, and their jurisdiction also extends to all cases arising under the revenue laws. They are also invested with jurisdiction of certain classes of cases removed to them, under special statutes, from the State Courts; including suits between citizens of different States, suits against aliens, and suits and prosecutions against military and other officers of the Government. The Circuit Courts entertain appeals from the District Courts in criminal cases, and in civil cases where the matter in dispute exceeds the sum of fifty dollars.

III. The United States is further divided into districts, for the holding of U.S. District Courts therein. A district usually includes a single State; but the larger States are divided into two or sometimes three districts. For each district there is a District Judge, who holds four regular sessions of the District Court annually. The salaries of the District Judges are different in different parts of the country. The District Courts have original and exclusive jurisdiction of admiralty and maritime cases, of cases of seizures on land and water, under the laws of the United States, and of suits brought for penalties and forfeitures incurred under said laws. They have also jurisdiction, exclusive of the State Courts, of suits against consuls, vice-consuls, etc. They have also concurrent jurisdiction with the Circuit Courts in cases of crimes and offences, not capital, committed under the laws of the United States. Also concurrent jurisdiction with such courts and the State Courts of suits at common law, in which the United States, or any officer thereof, may sue, under the authority of any law of the United States. Also a similar jurisdiction of all suits by aliens, on account of (torts) in violation of the laws of nations or a treaty of the United States.

IV. The Court of Claims sits in the Capital at Washington, and commences its regular annual session on the same day as the Supreme Court. . . . It consists of a Chief Justice and four Justices, with a salary of four thousand dollars each. It has jurisdiction of "all claims founded upon any law of Congress, or upon any regulation of an executive department, or upon any contract, express or implied, with the Government of the United States, which may be suggested to it by a petition filed therein, and also all claims which may be referred to said court by either House of Congress." [The Court of Claims also has] jurisdiction of all counter-claims and demands, on the part of the United States, against any persons making claim against the Government in said court; also jurisdiction of claims to property captured or abandoned during the rebellion; also jurisdiction of the claims of disbursing officers of the United States for relief from responsibility on account of losses of public property by capture or otherwise while in the line of duty; and of some other claims of less general importance. The court is precluded from passing upon claims for supplies taken, injuries done, etc., by United States troops during the rebellion, and from rendering judgment in favor of any claimant who has not been loyal to the United States. Appeals may be taken by the United States to the Supreme Court in all cases where the judgment is adverse to the United States; and by the claimant where the amount in controversy exceeds three thousand dollars. This court is the only court of the U.S. in which the United States can be directly sued as a defendant.

V. The Supreme Court of the District of Columbia consists of a Chief Justice and three other Justices, and holds its sessions at the City Hall in Washington. The salary of the Chief Justice is four thousand five hundred dollars, and of each of the other Justices four thousand dollars. This court combines the general powers and jurisdiction of a Circuit Court and a District Court. Any single one of its judges is authorized to hold a District Court. Its jurisdiction extends only to civil proceedings instituted, and crimes committed, in the District of Columbia; and to cases of seizures on land and water made, and penalties and forfeitures incurred, under the laws of the United States within the same limits only. It entertains appeals from the local justices of the peace and police courts; and its final judgments, orders, and decrees are subject to be appealed from to the Supreme Court of the United States.

VI. Territorial Courts. When a territorial government is organized by Congress for any Territory, a judiciary is provided, consisting generally of a Supreme Court of three or more judges, District Courts, to be held by the Judges of the Supreme Court separately, Probate Courts, and Justices' Courts. The District Courts are invested with the jurisdiction of the Circuit and District Courts of the United States; and an appeal is given from the District Courts to the Supreme Court. An appeal is also provided from the Supreme Court to the Supreme Court of the United States, in the same manner as from a Circuit Court. When a Territory is admitted into the Union as a State, these courts cease to exist, being supplanted by the State Courts.

Final Thoughts on America[1]

Now that this little book is finished, the mind of the compiler naturally turns to take a single comprehensive view of the great country which has been briefly described. It is, indeed, one of the wonders of the century and of the world. The extent of its domain and its unbounded resources, the peaceful blending of its many nationalities, the well-nigh unlimited diffusion of intelligence and knowledge, and the free, cosmopolitan character of its people, combine to give it a conspicuous position among the nations. At the very moment when these closing lines are being written, a Diplomatic Embassy [the Iwakura embassy] from the Tenno [emperor] of Japan is on the point of visiting the city of Washington, and the fact cannot but have made an impression on their minds, that, after landing on the soil of America, they have been compelled to travel more than three thousand miles before reaching the metropolis. But when the Ambassadors, and the other high officials who accompany them, are informed as to the warm welcome which is in store for them from the Government of the United States, and many of the leading men and corporations throughout the Union, and when they shall have experienced the unbounded hospitality of the American people generally, they will undoubtedly be deeply impressed, and effectually convinced that America and Japan are strongly bound together by the cords of sincere regard and unselfish affection.

---

1. This section was originally titled "Additional Notes" and included two updated paragraphs on religious and educational life, and one updated paragraph on agricultural production. These paragraphs have been moved to the end of the chapters on those subjects.

Appendix One

"Religious Freedom in Japan"

A Memorial and Draft of Charter

To His Excellency.

SANJO SANEYOSHI [SANETOMI]

Prime Minister in His Imperial Majesty's Government[1]

Sir:

Among many important human concerns, the one respecting our religious faith appears to be the most vital. In all the enlightened nations of the earth, the liberty of conscience, especially in matters of religious faith, is sacredly regarded as not only an inherent right of man, but also as a most fundamental element to advance all human interests.

It is a strange and grievous fact that we fail to find in the whole history of the long and glorious continuance of our intelligent race, a trace of the recognition in any form of this sacred right. It is even more remarkable, amid the wonderful progress we now behold, that our people are not as yet quite earnest and thorough in their consideration of this important subject.

To those who have been brought up in the strange school of that political economy which advocates the superior excellence of ignorance over knowledge for all the governed, as well as to those who believe in the senseless precept of *simplicity or the natural state,* such doctrines as the rights of man or the liberty of conscience may appear as something strange and dreadful. Even

---

1. Court noble who helped anti-Tokugawa forces "restore" imperial rule in 1868, Sanjo Sanetomi (1838–1891) became a major leader during the early years of the Meiji government. Sanjo served as *dajō daijin*, the top minister in the Council of State system that existed from 1868 to 1885. However, other ministers in the Meiji government, especially Okubo Toshimichi (1830–1878), Okuma Shigenobu (1838–1922), and Ito Hirobumi (1841–1909) wielded the most power in the government.

our government may not find itself in a position practically to adopt these views. It has wisely to overcome all the influences of prejudice and ignorance, which are still blindly hostile to the light of the new idea.

The department specially established for the administration of our religious affairs, has indicated to the public as yet no mark of its success in gaining the confidence of the people. Far from it. Its policy of combining the two antagonistic faiths of Buddhism and Shintoism, which some time since was inaugurated under its sway, has utterly failed to command our respect. Its attempt to impose upon our people a religion of its creation cannot receive too severe condemnation, because such an attempt not only disregards our sacred liberty of conscience, but its effect is to crush the very soul of man. Every one that lives is himself solely responsible to his Creator for all his thoughts and deeds. He who is deprived of the knowledge of this responsibility, and the freedom to exercise it can no longer be rightly called a man in the proper sense of the term. The notion of making a new religion or precept by the authority of the State, which now prevails in our country, has a strange appearance in the light of reason. Religion can neither be sold to, nor forced upon, any one. It is, if set forth in a word, a duty of man as a rational being, and according to the internal conception of its light, we, independently of each other are enabled to know and to enjoy the happy life of faith, and insight into spiritual truth. One of the great beauties of nature is its abounding and inexhaustible variety. There is a corresponding beauty in the infinite variety existing in our mental and moral worlds. The array of various religious faiths is one of the most interesting and edifying spectacles that can be presented to the mind of man.

Religion undergoes changes from time to time, adapting itself to circumstances. "The religions we call false," observed Emerson, a profound American philosopher, "were once true. They also were affirmations of the conscience, correcting the evil customs of their times."[2]

It may be said in defense, that the necessity of our present situation demands action, for the protection of our people from the strange and fearful influences of the many new doctrines which now threaten to invade us from abroad. Our experience of Christian troubles in the past, warns us strongly against the faith from which they were supposed to have sprung, and while permitting an indulgence of the supposition that the Christian faith may contain something good and beneficial, it may be contended that we are not yet sufficiently prepared to allow its introduction because we are still incapable of discriminating between the good and the bad. It is generally believed to embrace so many evils and superstitions that the very name of Christianity is,

---

2. Ralph Waldo Emerson (1803–1882), well-known American author, philosopher, and leader in the transcendentalist movement.

in the popular estimation, almost identical with those bad qualities just described. These objections are urged by one class against Christianity and another class denounce it as dangerous to our national constitution because its introduction will produce a sad discord between superiors and inferiors in our class system of society.[3] And, finally, there will be others who will argue, in a submissive manner, against its immediate introduction, because it will be likely to involve some unnecessary disturbance, and thus retard our progress. Other objections might be raised; but it is believed that those of the gravest kind have been described.

Let me now proceed to reply to them, and try to show how unreasonable and·worthless they will all prove.

The objections first mentioned rest on the notion that the Christian religion is bad and superstitious. If it were good and perfect no opposition to its introduction or invasion could exist. There is no better way of indicating the absurd character of this objection than that of asking the question [of] whether those who oppose Christianity have any knowledge of its character?

The prevalent notion that it is wrong to allow the Christian faith to come into the Empire without discriminating between its good and bad qualities, appears to be much more unreasonable than the objection just referred to, when we inquire who can be found with the requisite authority to perform the awful and responsible duty of separating the good from the evil. To dare to undertake the task one should possess qualities essentially equal to those of Christ himself. Let him discriminate if he please in his own case, but not for another person who may not have given him authority so to do. He cannot possibly assume to decide for another, without committing a serious crime of violence upon the right of the other. Nor can any government perform this service without prostituting its sacred office to one of transgression. The protection of the people in their proper rights is one of the most important among the many grave responsibilities with which the government is charged. To practice violence against our inherent rights of conscience is not one of the purposes for which it has been created.

The second objection is raised from a needless fear that the introduction of Christianity will produce discord in our social relations. Progress without revolution is impossible. A discord in society is often a blessing. The question therefore stands whether the anticipated discord would prove to be one of injury or of blessing. The answer cannot, either socially or politically, be

---

3. By "national constitution" Mori meant the social and political structure of Japan, not a written document of basic laws for the nation, which would be enacted in 1889. The class system was the warriors/peasants/artisans/merchants Confucian-oriented, heredity system that had only recently been abolished.

otherwise than that it would decidedly be a blessing, because the society which receives the addition of a new knowledge, and a power of the character of the Christian morality and faith, will necessarily better its condition by becoming both wiser and stronger. This is no mere assertion. It is fact, demonstrated by the history of the nations of the earth, among which none have so grandly advanced to the head of civilization as those whose religion has been Christianity. However injurious and fearful it may temporally appear, the evidence of the benefits of such a polity will sooner or later accustom opponents to its adoption in the ratio of their better acquaintance with the true philosophy of social improvement and political progress. Since religion is entirely a matter of individual belief, no one or government can be presumed to possess the authority of repudiating whatever faith any man may cherish within himself. And the facts place beyond dispute the averments that none of us, either high or low by political institution, is different one from another in human organization; and that, irrespective of our class organization of society, nature or the Creator distributes human qualities unequally among us, and therefore it cannot be expected that all will take the same view of such a question. It may with propriety be remarked here that no man or society of men is in the least entitled to assume the power of dictating the thought and action of the sovereign or any other person without committing a grievous wrong. It is painful to observe that this enormity is too often practiced among those who hold despotism above the right principles of humanity. It may be noted that these wrong-doers generally style themselves, either ignorantly or craftily, as the most faithful in discharging duties to their country.

The third and last objection is entirely based upon precaution against any tendency to disturbance, resulting from an immediate introduction of Christianity.

In all matters we deal with, true precaution is important, nay, absolutely essential. The precaution that we exercise in accomplishing a difficult purpose is a part of the action, and is an assistance in reaching the result. The precaution that forbids an attempt to undertake the task is not precaution; it is rather neglect. The precaution suggested in the objection partakes of the last-described character. This kind of precaution, signifying inattention, or, correctly speaking, negligence, is truly a wall against progress. It fails to answer its purpose, and therefore should be turned in another and better direction, and become an active and protecting element of progress.

The best and most practical precautions for progress are as follows: The establishment of proper laws by which all the proper rights of man shall be recognized and protected from violence; and the organization of an educational system by which the whole condition of our people shall be so elevated that their moral strength will sufficiently protect their rights, even without the additional dry and unsatisfactory shield of the written law of the state.

The established laws should secure a complete liberty of conscience. First, by a sufficient protection for the free exercise of that liberty in matters of religion, so far as its outward action does not conflict with the law of the state. Second, by a perfect impartiality in the attitude of the state in relation to all religious denomination. Third, by the protection from disturbances which may arise from disagreement in their religious faith and formulas. In consideration of these points the paper accompanying this address, and bearing the title of "Religious Charter of the Empire of Dai Nippon," has been prepared as a draft, and is now humbly submitted to your distinguished attention.

It must be remembered that progress can only be achieved through revolutions and trials, inasmuch as such is the law of nature. The benefits of social revolution have been amply experienced by our people now for many centuries, especially within the last twenty years. Who will deny this plain fact? We should, moreover, be fully aware that indifference to such an important and vital human interest as religious liberty is, in fact, to silently sanction the perpetuation of a practice of violence upon the sacred rights of man. Against such an indignity let us firmly and resolutely stand, even to the sacrifice of our life, so that our nation may live without crime. Yea, let the law be speedily established to secure for us all our inalienable rights. It will be injurious to none to perpetuate the good, and rectify the bad. The best laws are the safest guide for both the governing and the governed. The governor, under such circumstances, has the best prerogative, and the governed the fullest liberty.

I venture now to indicate what I consider as the other but more important element of the precautions for progress, namely, an educational organization by which we shall secure all our rights. While the laws are the best protection for our liberty, its greatest security depends wholly upon the character and potency of our popular education. The value and urgency of an interest in education is at once manifest. Every one of us must be profoundly convinced that our present position is one of awful responsibility. We are charged with the task of moulding the destiny of our nation. Nay, more, the influence we shall exert cannot fail to have its fruit in the initiation of similar laws in all other nations of Asia. It is of the utmost importance that we should with full force and great solemnity hasten forward in the right direction, and with herculean zeal endeavor to do our best, in the great cause of humanity.

No civilization, or enlightened state of human society can be attained, so long as we remain beneath our proper degree of manhood. It has justly been illustrated by the renowned Horace Mann, one of the most distinguished American characters and a most eminent writer on education, in the following expression: "As an apple is not in any proper sense an apple until it is ripe,

so a human being is not in any proper sense a human being until he is educated." Another sagacious and emphatic word by the same great personage
may not less appropriately be quoted: "Education," says he, "is our only political safety; outside of this ark all is deluge."

Let me now for a moment dwell upon the character and scope of the proposed educational organization. A few words are sufficient to indicate generally what I have in my mind in relation to [it]. The principal characteristic
[should be] an entire absence of any particular religious influence. The scope
should comprehend universal learning, and include all classes and kinds of
persons without distinction and with perfect impartiality.

Since it has already been amply stated in these pages that religious faiths
are purely matters of individual conviction, and cannot be subject to any political authority, it need hardly be added that it is wrong for the State to usurp,
as a function within its province, the introduction of religious influences into
the educational administration. There are those who are opposed to the interference of the State in any affairs of education. These persons hold that it may
reasonably be asserted that education is entirely a subject for personal and
private determination. I have no desire to oppose such a view, so long as parents or guardians are faithful to their trust.

If the State has any authority at all to punish criminals, or, correctly speaking, to protect its people from violence, it certainly has equal authority to assure their peace. No, the State cannot possibly disclaim its responsibility [to
promote education]. It can best discharge its obligations by assisting in the
diffusion of a knowledge of facts in science and art, and thus it shall establish
peace upon a solid foundation of enlightenment, and let the base influence of
ignorance—the source of all human miseries—perish through its own weak-
ness as speedily as possible.

By the diffusion of knowledge among the people it is not intended to confine the spread of information to any special class or kind, but to extend it so
that every one, whether male or female, without exception, shall be its recip-
ients. The mode of giving every one in the community an opportunity to receive an education may vary according to his or her condition in regard to age
and occupations. It is not necessary in this paper to discuss details; but it is
sufficient to say that every possible means that can be adapted to the circumstances should be employed to advance all kinds of useful knowledge for the
general improvement of our entire people.

Let our nation be an apt scholar, and soon it may be its lot to wait upon
other nations as their beneficial educator, as well as their agreeable associate
in living the life of happiness and true grandeur.

Before concluding this paper, permit me, Sir, to express my sincere hope
that you will be disposed to consider seriously its important subject, and that

you will be able to make such disposition of it and the accompanying draft of a "Religious Charter of Japan" as will be best calculated to serve the public interest.

If in the course of the preceding remarks, there appears anything which, contrary to my expectations, may possibly be offensive, I must humbly yet firmly assure you that it occurs, not from any want of respect or loyalty, but is a result of the excess of my intense solicitude for the interests and happiness of my country and her people

I have the honor, Sir, to be yours

Most respectfully,
MORI ARINORI.

Washington, D.C., U.S.A.
The 5th year of Meiji and the 25th of the 10th month. November 25, 1872.

Appendix Two

"The Religious Charter of the Empire of Dai Nippon"

Whereas, in matters of conscience and religious faith, it has been justly observed that the manner of exercising them can be properly determined only by reason and conviction, not by force or violence, and

Whereas, no man or society of men has any right to impose his or its opinions or interpretations on any other in matters of religion, since every man must be responsible for himself, and

Whereas, we have no other purpose than that of avoiding for our nation the misery which the experience of the world shows has followed the patronage, by the State, of any particular religion,

It is now solemnly resolved and declared that the Imperial Government of Dai Nippon will make no law prohibiting, either directly or indirectly, the free exercise of conscience or religious liberty within its dominions.

And it is further solemnly resolved and declared that the organization of any religious order shall not be interfered with by either local or national authority, so long as such organization does not conflict with the laws of the State.

And it is further solemnly resolved and declared that the law of the Empire shall recognize no religious institution as special or different from any other kind of social institution.

And it is further solemnly resolved and declared that no special privilege or favor shall be granted by either local or national authority to any particular sect or religious denomination, without extending the same at once to every other.

And it is further solemnly resolved and declared that no religious or ecclesiastical title or rank shall be conferred by the State upon any person belonging to any religious association.

And it is further, and in conclusion, solemnly resolved and declared that no action which may promote religious animosity shall be permitted with the realm.[1]

---

1. Official prohibitions against Christianity and the spreading of Christian beliefs, which began in the late sixteenth century, were repealed by the Meiji government in 1873. While Mori did play a major role in the repeal of these prohibitions, his "Religious Charter" was never adopted by the government.

Selected Bibliography

There is a significant and growing number of works on Japan in the nineteenth century, including its relations with the United States. Below are listed only those works cited in the foreword, the introduction, and the annotations to *Life and Resources in America*, and other works most directly related to Mori Arinori and/or Japan in the 1860s and 1870s.

Abe, Yoshiya. "From Prohibition to Toleration: Japanese Government Views Regarding Christianity, 1854–1873." *Japanese Journal of Religious Studies*, Vol. 5, Nos. 2–3 (1978).

Asao, Naohiro. *Sakoku*. Tokyo: Shogakkan, 1975.

Beasely, W. G. *Japan Encounters the Barbarian: Japanese Travellers in America and Europe*. New Haven: Yale University Press, 1995.

——. *The Meiji Restoration*. Stanford: Stanford University Press, 1972.

——, ed. *Select Documents on Japanese Foreign Policy, 1853–1868*. Oxford: Oxford University Press, 1955.

Beauchamp, Edward R., and Akira Iriye, eds. *Foreign Employees in Nineteenth Century Japan*. Boulder: Westview Press, 1990.

Braisted, William R., ed. and trans. *Meiroku Zasshi: Journal of the Japanese Enlightenment*. Cambridge, Mass.: Harvard University Press, 1976.

Burks, Ardath, ed. *The Modernizers: Overseas Students, Foreign Employees, and Meiji Japan*. Boulder: Westview Press, 1985.

Chan, Sucheng. *This Bittersweet Soil: The Chinese in California Agriculture, 1860–1910*. Berkeley: University of California Press, 1986.

Craig, Albert M. *Choshu in the Meiji Restoration*. Lanham, Md.: Lexington Books, 2000. Originally published: Cambridge, Mass.: Harvard University Press, 1961.

Cobbing, Andrew. *The Satsuma Students in Britain: Japan's Early Search for the Essence of the West*. London: Japan Library, Curzon Press, 2000.

Daniels, Roger. *The Politics of Prejudice: The Anti-Japanese Movement in California and the Struggle for Japanese Exclusion*, 2nd edition. Berkeley: University of California Press, 1977.

Davidann, Jon Thares. *A World of Crisis and Progress: The American YMCA in Japan, 1890–1930*. Bethlehem, Pa.: Lehigh University Press, 1998.

Duus, Peter, ed. *The Japanese Discovery of America*. Boston: Bedford Books, 1997.

Ericsom, Jack, ed. *Thomas Lake Harris and the Brotherhood of the New Life: Books, Pamphlets, Serials, and Manuscripts*. Glen Rock, N.J.: Microfilming Corporation of America, 1974.

Fujitani, T. *Splendid Monarchy: Power and Pageantry in Modern Japan*. Berkeley: University of California Press, 1996.

Fukuzawa, Yukichi. *The Autobiography of Yukichi Fukuzawa*. Eiichi Kiyooka, trans. New York: Columbia University Press, 1960.

Gluck, Carol. *Japan's Modern Myths: Ideology in the Late Meiji Period*. Princeton, N.J.: Princeton University Press, 1985.

Goodman, Grant. *Japan: The Dutch Experience*. London: Athelone Press, 1986.

Handlin, Oscar, and Lilian Handlin, eds. *From the Outer World*. Cambridge, Mass.: Harvard University Press, 1996.

Hall, Ivan Parker. *Mori Arinori*. Cambridge, Mass.: Harvard University Press, 1973.

Hane, Mikiso. "Early Meiji Liberalism: An Assessment." *Monumenta Nipponica*, Vol. 24, No. 4 (1969).

Hardy, Arthur S., ed. *Life and Letters of Joseph Hardy Neesima*. Boston and New York: Houghton Mifflin and Company, 1891.

Harootunian, Harry D. *Toward Restoration*. Berkeley: University of California Press, 1970.

Hawks, Francis L. *Narrative of the Expedition of an American Squadron to the China Seas and Japan*. New York: D. Appleton and Company, 1857.

Hayashi, Takeji. *Mori Arinori*. Tokyo: Chikuma Shobo, 1986.

Henning, Joseph M. *Outposts of Civilization: Race, Religion, and the Formative Years of American–Japanese Relations*. New York: New York University Press, 2000.

Hirakawa, Sukehiro. "Japan's Turn to the West." *The Cambridge History of Japan, Vol. 5, The Nineteenth Century*. Marius Jansen, ed. Cambridge: Cambridge University Press, 1989.

Inuzuka, Takaaki. *Mori Arinori*. Tokyo: Yoshikawa Kobunkan, 1986.

——. *Satsumahan Eikoku Ryugakusei*. Tokyo: Chuo Koronsha, 1974.

Iriye, Akira. *Across the Pacific: An Inner History of American–East Asian Relations*. New York: Harcourt, Brace, Jovanovich, 1967.

——. "Japan's Drive to Great Power Status." *The Cambridge History of Japan, Vol. 5, The Nineteenth Century*. Marius Jansen, ed. Cambridge: Cambridge University Press, 1989.

——, ed. *Mutual Images: Essays in American–Japanese Relations*. Cambridge, Mass.: Harvard University Press, 1975.

Ishizuki, Minoru. *Kindai Nihon no Kaigai Ryugakusei*. Rev. ed. Tokyo: Chuo Koronsha, 1992.

Jansen, Marius. *Sakamoto Ryoma and the Meiji Restoration*. Princeton, N.J.: Princeton University Press, 1961.

Japan Government, Agency for Cultural Affairs. *Japanese Religion.* Tokyo: Kodansha International, Ltd., 1972.

Kadota, Paul Akira, and Terry Earl Jones. *Kanaye Nagasawa: A Biography of a Satsuma Student.* Kagoshima, Japan: Kagoshima Prefectural Junior College, 1990.

Keene, Donald. *Emperor of Japan: Meiji and His World, 1852–1912.* New York: Columbia University Press, 2002.

Kido, Takayoshi. *The Diary of Kido Takayoshi,* 3 vols. Translated by Sidney Brown and Akiko Hirota. Tokyo: University of Tokyo Press, 1983 and 1985.

Kume, Kunitake, comp. *The Iwakura Embassy, 1871–73,* 5 vols., Graham Healy and Chushichi Tsuzuki, eds. Surrey, UK, and Princeton, N.J.: Princeton University Press, 2002.

Kuno, Akiko. *Unexpected Destinations: The Poignant Story of Japan's First Vassar Graduate.* Tokyo: Kodansha International, 1993.

Lanman, Charles. *Leaders of the Meiji Restoration in America.* Yoshiyuki Okamura, ed. Tokyo: Hokuseido Press, 1931.

——. *Leading Men of Japan.* Boston: D. Lothrop and Company, 1882.

——, and Arinori Mori. *The Japanese in America.* New York: University Publishing Company, 1872.

Lu, David. J. *Japan: A Documentary History.* 2 vols. New York: M. E. Sharpe, 1997.

Miyoshi, Masao. *As We Saw Them: The First Japanese Embassy to the United States.* Berkeley: University of California Press, 1979.

Mori, Arinori. *Education in Japan: A Series of Letters Addressed by Prominent Americans to Arinori Mori.* New York: D. Appleton, 1873.

——. *Life and Resources in America.* Washington, D.C.: n.p., 1871.

——. "Religious Freedom in Japan: A Memorial and Draft of Charter." Washington, D.C.: n.p., November 1872.

Muragaki, Awaji no kami. *Kokkai Nikki: The Diary of the First Japanese Embassy to the United States.* Helen M. Uno, trans. Tokyo: Foreign Affairs Association of Japan, 1958.

Nagai, Kafu. *American Stories.* Mitsuko Iriye, trans. New York: Columbia University Press, 2000.

Nagasawa, Kanaye. "The Diaries of Kanaye Nagasawa," Gaye LeBaron, ed. *Kenkyu Nenpo.* No. 9. Kagoshima, Japan: Kagoshima Junior College, 1980.

Notehelfer, F. G., ed. *Japan through American Eyes: The Journal of Francis Hall, Kanagawa and Yokohama, 1859–1866.* Princeton, N.J.: Princeton University Press, 1992.

Okubo, Toshiaki, ed. *Mori Arinori Zenshu.* 3 vols. Tokyo: Seibundo, 1971–1973.

——, Hachiro Kaminuma, and Takaaki Inuzuka, eds. *Shinshu Mori Arinori Zenshu.* 6 vols. Tokyo: Bunsendo Shoten, 1997–1999.

Rose, Barbara. *Tsuda Umeko and Women's Education in Japan.* New Haven: Yale University Press, 1992.

Sakamaki, Shunzo. *Japan and the United States, 1790–1853.* Tokyo: The Asiatic Society of Japan, 1939; reprint, Wilmington, Del.: Scholarly Resources, Inc., 1973.

Sakamoto, Moriaki. *Mori Arinori no Shiso.* Tokyo: Jiji Tsushinsha, 1969.

Samsom, George. *The Western World and Japan: A Study in the Interaction of European and Asiatic Cultures.* New York: Alfred A. Knopf, 1950.

Samuels, Richard. *Rich Nation, Strong Army: National Security and the Technological Transformation of Japan*. Ithaca, N.Y.: Cornell University Press, 1994.

Scheiner, Irwin. *Christian Converts and Social Protest in Meiji Japan*. Berkeley: University of California Press, 1970.

Schneider, Herbert, and George Lawton. *A Prophet and a Pilgrim*. New York: Columbia University Press, 1942.

Smith, Thomas C. *Native Sources of Japanese Industrialization, 1750–1920*. Berkeley: University of California Press, 1988.

Swale, Alistair. *The Political Thought of Mori Arinori: A Study in Meiji Conservatism*. London: Japan Library, Curzon Press, 2000.

Toby, Ronald. *State and Diplomacy in Early Modern Japan: Asia in the Development of the Tokugawa Bakufu*. 2nd edition. Stanford: Stanford University Press, 1991.

Tocqueville, Alexis de. *Democracy in America*. Harvey Mansfield and Debra Winthrop, eds. Chicago: University of Chicago Press, 2000.

Totman, Conrad. *The Collapse of the Tokugawa Bakufu, 1862–1868*. Honolulu: University of Hawaii Press, 1980.

Tsurumi, Patricia. *Factory Girls: Women in the Thread Mills of Meiji Japan*. Princeton, N.J.: Princeton University Press, 1990.

Umegaki, Michio. *After the Restoration: The Beginning of Japan's Modern State*. New York: New York University Press, 1988.

United States Government, Department of State. *Foreign Relations of the United States, 1868–69*. Washington, D.C.: Government Printing Office, 1870.

Van Sant, John E. *Pacific Pioneers: Japanese Journeys to America and Hawaii, 1850–1880*. Urbana and Chicago: University of Illinois Press, 2000.

Walker, Brett. "Reappraising the Sakoku Paradigm." *Journal of Asian History*, Vol. 30, No. 2 (1996).

Watanabe, Minoru. *Niijima Jo*. Tokyo: Yoshikawa Kobunkan, 1959.

Index